THE GOD OF SECOND CHANCES

THE GOD
OF SECOND CHANCES

Erik Kolbell

Westminster John Knox Press
LOUISVILLE • LONDON

Scripture quotations from the New Revised Standard Version of the Bible are copyright © 1989 by the Division of Christian Education of the National Council of the Churches of Christ in the U.S.A. and are used by permission.

Lyrics from "Attics of My Life" by Robert Hunter, copyright © Ice Nine Publishing Company. Used with permission.

Book design by Sharon Adams
Cover design by Jennifer K. Cox

First edition
Published by Westminster John Knox Press
Louisville, Kentucky

This book is printed on acid-free paper that meets the American National Standards Institute Z39.48 standard. ♾

PRINTED IN THE UNITED STATES OF AMERICA

08 09 10 11 12 13 14 15 16 17 — 10 9 8 7 6 5 4 3 2 1

Library of Congress Cataloging-in-Publication Data

Kolbell, Erik.
    The God of second chances / Erik Kolbell. — 1st ed.
      p. cm.
  ISBN 978-0-664-23122-4 (alk. paper)
  1. Christian life. 2. Spirituality. 3. Christianity. 4. Failure (Psychology)
—Religious aspects—Christianity. 5. Guilt—Religious aspects—Christianity. I. Title.
  BV4501.3.K65 2008
  248.4—dc22

                                  2007041808

To my sister, Karen, and my brother, Richard.
Despite any evidence to the contrary, I love you both.

Contents

Preface

*Adam was but human—this explains it all. He did not want
the apple for the apple's sake, he wanted it only because it
was forbidden.*

—Mark Twain

*The deep moans round with many voices. Come, my friends,
'tis not too late to seek a newer world.*

—Tennyson

God does not make life easy for us, nor we for ourselves. Both Scripture and common sense bear this out. But he does endow us with both the opportunity and the wherewithal not only to endure life but to correct our mistakes, overcome our challenges, repent our sins, and repair the damages they evince. To paraphrase Gandhi, we humans are drops in that limitless ocean of God's mercy. Ours is a God of second chances.

When we see our own stories mirrored in the likes of Adam and Eve, who fell from grace but then gave birth to human civilization, or Paul, a persecutor of the early church who became its greatest advocate, we recognize that our relationship with God is one of exile and restoration; of wandering and returning, coming back; of picking ourselves up where we have fallen, accepting the divine second chance, and trying again to live in concert with our higher angels rather than our lower impulses. The journey is down a well-worn road, and when we are on it, chastened, and coming back home to God, we inevitably stumble upon the footprints we left when we headed off in the other direction. We vow that those errant prints will always remind us to point ourselves Godward. But of course they do not, and neither do we. Inevitably, we go off again. Such is our life of faith. It is a life of the prodigal, the one who has wandered off in search of a better deal, but who is ultimately looking to go back again, make confession, make amends, and start anew. Whether, upon returning, he or she stays, is never certain.

This movement to and from God, while a personal gesture, can also be a communal one, for entire cultures, as well as smaller groups within those cultures, can suffer the same sense of alienation as the individuals within them. That alienation might come in the form of a family whose members have, through inattentiveness, lost their love of one another, or a church divided because one group's moral imperative is another's heresy. It can come in the form of a nation that was founded on principles of freedom and justice but that has slowly sacrificed those principles to the gods of militarism, classism, and political expediency. Whatever the form, whatever the circumstances, whatever the cast of characters, I believe it is in our nature to slip away from Elysian harmony, just as it is in God's nature—as both a stern and loving parent—to call us back to it.

Why Now?

Perhaps it is a narrow view of history on my part, but it is my impression that we have slipped further away from God in recent years than in years past. Our culture is tinged by religious intolerance. Our debates over pressing issues have lost whatever civil tone they once had and have become the purview of vitriol-spewing talk show hosts, the radio equivalent of professional smack-down wrestlers. Our nation is awash in multimillionaires and homeless children. Our government sends some citizens off to battle and spies on others here at home, both under the false pretense of fighting a war against nameless, faceless monsters about whom all we are told is that they are from another country and "they mean to do us harm." Now, in particular, we need a second chance.

Re-

Re- is a little Latin prefix that simply means to go back to, to do again. We *re*live the memory of a lover's first kiss or the joy of a child's first step. We *re*build the old farmhouse and the ancient stone wall that encircles it. We *re*connect with an old friend, *re*iterate an important point, and attend our college *re*union. We *re*new our charity pledge, our wedding vows, our magazine subscription, or our faith. We practice our *re*ligion, our *re legere*, meaning literally, "to read the stories again." It is no surprise that in reading those stories again we come upon words like *revival, repentance, reconciliation, remembrance, rejoice, redemption, resurrection.* They are our expressions of hope, each in its own way, that no matter how far we might wander from a truly integrated life, we can always find our way back, and when we do, we will be welcomed by our God of second chances.

I write this book to show how this theme of return is pertinent to our lives as spiritual seekers whose paths are not always even or easy, whose intentions are often nobler than our actions, who are quickly distracted, discouraged, or enticed away, but who want truly to dwell again in the sufficiency of God's love and who desire the wisdom to know what it is we must do with that love. In the words of the poet Denise Levertov, "the road unfurls itself, we don't stop walking, we know there is far to go." I believe that both Scripture and stories from our own lives show how, in so many situations, from the momentous to the mundane, God bids us to take this walk, knowing that we will not always return, will not always make it back, and that when we do, we will not always stay but will have to go and come back again. And yet *another* chance will then be given by the God whose mercy knows no bounds.

In these pages you will find repeated references to Job, or Paul, or Adam and Eve, or the ancient Hebrews, because in all of their stories I find much that speaks to the theme of this book. They are by no means the only examples of the second chance, but their stories often most clearly illustrate what that second chance looks like.

This book is a reflection of my own beliefs and musings; no one else must bear responsibility for either the words on these pages or the thoughts behind them. That said, it would not have come to fruition without the help of one very charitable man and four very strong and wise women, to whom I am indebted. In no particular order biblical scholar Marc Mullinay for his help with Greek and Hebrew. I thank my wife, Ann, for relieving me of all responsibilities foreign and domestic in the race to complete the manuscript. I also thank our daughter, Kate, for making sure that my feet and ego stayed anchored firmly to the ground. I am grateful to my agent, Claudia Cross, whose belief in the book was indispensable and whose belief in the author shows that generosity often outweighs reason. Finally I am very much obliged to Stephanie Egnotovich, editor nonpareil, whose work is all about second chances and whose clarity of thought and attention to detail not only protected the ideas embedded in these pages, but made them far more available to the mind's eye.

Chapter 1

Restoration

A corner draft fluttered the flame, and the white fever of temptation upswept its angel wings that cast a cruciform shadow.
—Boris Pasternak

*I*t was in May of 1972, Pentecost Sunday to be exact, an otherwise unremarkable spring day in the eternal city when a lone man by the name of Lazlo Toth walked into Saint Peter's Basilica in Rome and, armed with a hammer, a vengeance, and a very disturbed mind, delivered fifteen blows to the upper portions of Michelangelo's magnificent *La Pietà*. "I am the Christ!" he yelled in full-throated rage, and in just a few short moments one man's masterpiece was felled by another man's madness. Toth's attack was as fierce as it was senseless, and upon hearing the news, Christians wept openly over the assault on this icon of theirs. Meanwhile people of no religious affiliation wept too, over the assault on a frail treasure that is all of ours, a treasure that was the embodiment of beauty itself. Said one bystander who spoke for both camps, "Ah, the world. It is a little uglier tonight."

Some years later, long after a team of craftsmen had painstakingly restored her to her former elegance, a friend of mine, an art historian and practicing Catholic by the name of Tom Primeau, offered a more measured assessment. "It was good to get her back, but she's not the same, you know," he told me, with the kind of sadness in his voice we often reserve for the memories of a lost love or a dashed hope.

"She doesn't look much different," he went on, "and to the naked eye the scars are undetectable," he said. Then, after a long pause, he added, "but make no mistake about it, they're there." It began to dawn on me that Tom's words were coming more from his faith than his training.

"What really makes her different now is the fact that her history is different; now when we look at her we not only see the divine beauty that flowed like a river from the artist's hands to the marble itself, we also see the power of evil to destroy that beauty, to take it away from us, and to leave *us* permanently scarred as well. All art is a message, you know, and her message has changed." Indeed it has, I thought, particularly as I considered how that message is now shielded from us by a two-inch-thick wall of bulletproof Plexiglas—a kind of space-age sarcophagus, a tomb for the renaissance statue that spoke to us of the victory of life over death.

The story of *La Pietà*'s birth, death, and restoration has a fabulist quality to it, a sort of Aesop on a dark day. Everything seems to be representative—if in extremis—of some piece of the human condition. If Michelangelo is symbolically the divine expression of our goodness, Toth is, symbolically, the depths to which we are capable of sinking. The unnamed craftsmen who tend to her in exile, who bind her wounds, symbolize our desire to mend our destructive ways. The time that was given over to that repair is the time of exile, when we are separated from the divine form. Those who come back to see her again, scars and all, remind us that for all our imperfections we are still seekers of the good. Taken together, the moral of the story is that we have a sense of the perfect, what Plato called the Beautiful, and that we aspire to it. But, wanting to transcend the God-given constraints of our humanity, to "play god" ("I am the Christ!" Toth thundered), we fall away from it. Finally, wishing to restore what was, we do so, but only approximately.

The Primal Exile

As a morality tale, however, it predates even Aesop. It is as old as Eden itself, as old as the first beatings of the first human heart. After all, having found themselves in an earthly paradise, what did Adam and Eve do but look past the beauty with which God had surrounded them, play god by reaching for the one fruit in the garden that was God's alone, and in so doing destroy everything that had been given them?

We say they succumbed to temptation; indeed, we say that by their very act they defined temptation, and that they did. But they defined it not as simply the desire for something, the way a child desires a candy bar, or a puppy a bone; they defined it as a rejection of the very notion that desire itself should know any constraints. Indeed, desire itself was not on trial here, as evidenced by the fact that God had bestowed such an extravagance of pleasure on Adam and Eve. What Adam and Eve play out in their moment with the serpent is an urge to push beyond those bestowals, an urge so consuming it binds us to that lower impulse within us that blinds us to the higher grandeur around us.

They are our wants that we anoint as our rights, these urges. I think of a young girl I once counseled when I was a school chaplain. She was a bright but somewhat values-challenged high school senior whose consuming passion was acceptance to Harvard, not because it was a good school but, as she put it, "because it is *Harvard*." She was less in the market for knowledge than for status, and all that she thought would accrue thenceforth. College was her Eden, but Harvard was her fruit. So while most of her classmates—not necessarily as smart but at least better counseled—were looking for schools that would give them an education, she was looking for a place that would give her a pedigree. What really made me wince was that I saw in her the seeds of what I saw in full flower in another young person, Stuart, a freshly minted MBA.

Stuart was a few years older but no less clueless than the Harvard wannabe when he told me of the only two things in life he really coveted (his words): a corner office and a yacht. "Stuart," I told him, pulling chaplain's rank, "that business school should've taught you three things about your earthly worth. One is that it's a function of your riches. Two, it's a function of how honestly you come into those riches. And three, it's a function of what you *do* with those riches. I don't know that you got your money's worth out of that place because I'd say they got through to you on the first point but missed the next two." It did not make for a comfortable moment between us, but I

wished him well, silently hoped that one day he might divine the difference between wealth and worth, and may have suggested he might
want to see if Enron was hiring.

It need not be money or bragging rights that is our darker muse;
one person's indifference can be another's obsession. For some it
might be the lure of bought beauty, the Botox treatments and hair
transplants, the breast enlargements, liposuctions, and thigh reduc-
tions that are all part of America's $15 billion annual love affair with
cosmetic surgery. For others it is the priceless cachet that comes with
in-group status: the backstage pass, the honored place at the head
table, the presidential photo op, the seats on the 50-yard line, or the
invitation to the boar hunt. For still others it could also be something
as clichéd as the furtively smoked cigarette that makes the young boy
believe he is older than his years, or the midday tryst that makes his
mother believe she is younger than hers.

Lest the self-righteous among us forget, that compelling urge also
need not be so id-driven; it is even there in the inveterate do-gooder,
starved for attention, desperate to be recognized, let alone loved, who
will be all things to all people. He is the one who checks his ego at
the door and hangs the coats at the company Christmas party; he, the
perennial designated driver, the good-natured butt of all jokes, the one
who lends the money that will never be repaid, walks the neighbor's
dog in the rain, and forgives the trespasses of those who would not
forgive him. Even good deeds can have dark motives.

Neither is this hubris an affliction of individuals alone. Remember
the lessons of George Orwell's fantasy *Animal Farm*, set somewhere
in the English countryside, in which the farm's pigs lead a revolt
against humans and establish an egalitarian society for themselves. It
is only a matter of time, though, before the rules start bending to fit
the pleasures of the rulers at the expense of the ruled so that, at book's
end, the distinction between the elite pigs and the humans who once
oppressed them has been all but lost. When I think of this I cannot
help but bring to mind a nation as great as ours, founded on the high-
est principles of decency and democracy, that now has to explain to
the world community why it countenances the torture and indefinite
detention of political prisoners, the wiretapping of private telephone
conversations, and the death penalty. What, if not an unabated lust for

power, can explain our increasing resemblance to those tyrannies we have so long and nobly opposed?

The Contemporary Exile

That piece of Adam and Eve in all of us, that overriding, all-consuming craving to pursue the thing we lack and persuade ourselves we need—be it love, looks, or money; prestige, power, or a place in history—is what makes us count other people's blessings at the expense of our own. Even in those instances when the chase does yield the goods—when Harvard says yes—our satisfaction is short-lived because there will always be another high-hanging fruit to bedevil us. As Oscar Wilde wrote, "I can resist everything except temptation!" And this is what brings us to our exile. Exile is the dark, brooding place where we pay the price of our hubris, our unrestrained urges that we have wielded like Toth's hammer, the stinging blows that have been struck in defiance against God's will. It is the wrong side of the garden gate, where Eden is still within our sight but no longer within our reach.

When I imagine exile I do not conjure up terrible places of earthly horror—remember, even Icarus got to fly. My mind does not go to Doré's wailing souls drowning in the river Styx or Spiegelman's spectral postmodernist characters in *Maus*. Instead I think of how, when we have absorbed ourselves in the urge to slake our desires, others around us become either tools or impediments to our aims. As the Buddhist sage Baba Ram Dass once put it, "When a pickpocket sees a saint, he only sees the saint's pockets." We do not look *at* one another so much as *through* one another. Community breaks down because motives are doubted and rivalry—real or imagined—gets the better of collaboration. Altruism is looked at cynically, and tightfisted charity is bestowed with pity parading as grace. There is no such thing as a free lunch; everything carries a price. We all have a little pickpocket in us.

I imagine exile as a place where competition is king, where the grandeur of our desires is commensurate with the poverty of our values. In exile yesterday's David aspires to be tomorrow's Goliath, Little League managers run up the score because even nine-year-old kids should know now how tough the world is, and a good parking space is worth a fistfight. If I am middle class and live in exile I care more about the lushness of my lawn than about the pesticides I use to keep it that way, and I do not mind if my next-door neighbor is as jealous of my yard as I am of his house, which is larger than mine. I go to church to hear sermons about how the gospel ratifies my beliefs rather than shapes them, how the poor will always be with us, why masters must be good to their slaves and wives subservient to their husbands. I read an ad in a magazine that invites me to save a child's life or turn the page. I turn the page.

Exile is our place of separation. It is the void in the basilica where the sculpture once stood; it is less the presence of evil than evil's aftermath—the absence of the beautiful. We are not tortured so much as we are alienated, distanced from the pure and the good. (Indeed, *ex ile* literally means "to wander away.") What matters then is not where we have wandered to or even how we got there but what we will do with our newfound circumstances. Think again of Adam and Eve; when they were cast out they were told that life was going to be very different, and very difficult, but they got on with things. They fended for themselves, found their way, learned how to survive, and began a family to which we are all heirs. To paraphrase Aeschylus, people in exile must feed on the dreams of hope.

Or consider Gerry. I have known him peripherally for over twenty-five years. His early adult years, consisting as they did of little more than a modest job and a small circle of friends, were, by his own reckoning, "unexceptional bordering on prosaic." But somewhere along the line Gerry got the entrepreneurial urge, and instead of satisfying it by learning how to sell real estate or Tupperware, he decided to build a methamphetamine lab in the basement of his home. Suffice it to say this was Gerry's forbidden fruit, the price of which was seven years in exile at a correctional facility in southern Oregon.

"At first I was just angry, and I directed my anger at everybody and everything except myself," he told me. "I was pissed off at the cops because I decided they had it in for me. Then I blamed my attorney for not defending me better. Then it was the judge for throwing the book at me, then my cellmates, the guards, blah, blah, blah. And then finally it dawned on me. I was in prison. This was my situation. It was of my own doing. I could kick at it all I wanted, or I could simply accept the fact that this is where my behavior had landed me, make the most of it, learn from it, and get on with my life."

I do not know if Gerry appreciated the theological underpinnings of what he said, but the truth is, recognition is the prologue to restoration. We are offered a glimpse of what once was, of the sculpture before the assault, and we are ready to go back. Scripture shows us this, shows us that with every disobedience that ends in exile God calls us back. After Eden there was the birth of civilization, and after the flood, the rainbow. After the tower of Babel and the scattering of people "abroad across the face of the earth," God called Abraham to a covenant, and the promise that from him would come a nation of descendants more numerous than the stars in the heavens. Years later, after God kept this promise with the Israelites but they broke theirs with him and were plunged into exile at the hands of the Babylonians, they still received from God the assurance that one day he would "plant them upon their land, and they shall never again be plucked up" (Amos 9:15). Again, he was good to his word. Divine patience will always outlast mortal impertinence.

Whatever the seduction that lured us into exile, what lures us out could as easily come in the form of a whisper as a shout. Gerry's was a quiet awakening, the kind of enlightenment that comes like a lazy dawn on a summer's day. The eyes see clearly but gradually. The body rises to meet the sun, and slowly warms as the evening's cold dissipates in the brightening sky. The mind freshens, clarifies, and the spirit lifts with the gentle hint of a new possibility, a new way of understanding things.

On the other hand, twenty-five hundred years ago and half a world away from what we now call Portland, Oregon, a Sakya prince by the name of Gautama, who had been sheltered from the world by doting parents, had a very different awakening. It was not until he was in his late twenties that Sakya first ventured forth from the comfort of his father's kingdom and encountered human suffering. This single experience so wrenched the young man that he abruptly left the kingdom, renounced his life of sybaritic ease, became an ascetic, and, in his moment of enlightenment beneath his Bodhi tree, took on the name of Buddha, or "Awakened One." Buddha's life from that point on was one of renunciation, restoration, and instruction.

For those of us who have been neither prisoner nor prince the recognition may come in a very different way. It might be the birth of a child or the death of a parent, a cautionary tale told by an old friend, or a lesson we learn on a uniquely profound study retreat. Or it could be brought on simply by the gradual realization that the pleasures I once aspired to with such singleness of mind have begun to lose their luster, and so one day I decide that I would rather love my neighbor than have him envy my lawn. Whatever the medium through which God comes to us, the message is the same. It is to come back, restore a sense of balance to our lives, a sense of gratitude to God for what we have and generosity to others for what they do not have. In Judaism the term is *Tikkun Olam*, which means "repair the world." It is the notion that the world is like a broken vessel, and each good deed that we do puts one shard of that vessel back where it belongs, so that if enough good deeds are done the world will be restored.

But just as exile is not hell on earth, restoration is not heaven. When we are "good with God" we are not by extension immunized from pain so much as we are protected from the consuming cynicism that can accompany that pain. When I think of human beings managing adversity with godly grace, I think of an old friend named Burt.

Burt was an indefatigable leftie from the old war-resistor movement, celebrating his eighty-eighth year on earth, when cancer paid an unwelcome visit and coursed its way through his sinuous little body. It was a war he could not resist and would not win.

On a hospital visit one night, near the end, having just read to him Psalm 133—his favorite—I bent down low over his bedside and asked him, "So Burt, how are you doing tonight?"

"I'm great!" he answered. "In fact, I'm all healed." Then, after a pause, he added, with a hint of sparkle shining through baby-blue eyes long since occluded by age, "I'll be dying soon. But I'm all healed!"

I loved that line; it was so Burt. There he lay, hooked up to wires and tubes and oxygen and drips seeping God knows what into his body, barely able to move his arms or speak above a whisper, telling me he was healed.

I believe he *was* healed, though, because I believe what he meant went to the very core of the word, because healing is rooted in the Old English *hælen*, which simply means "whole." Burt was dying. But Burt was whole.

His cancer odyssey had taken him through the many stages of dying, until, near the end, he was quite ready to go. He had said his goodbyes, made peace with God, and inventoried a life that, in his words, had been well lived. His pain was under control, his bills were paid, his emotional and logistical bags were packed. There were no loose fragments waiting to be tied up, no amnesties to be asked for or granted, no fight to be waged, no miracle cures to try. Burt was healed insofar as he was whole, complete, finished with his work here on earth. If I have ever seen anybody who was good with the God he believed he would soon meet it was Burt. Death would be his homecoming, his final restoration. At his funeral, the old Shaker hymn "How Can I Keep from Singing" was sung. What better sendoff, I thought, than these two verses:

> While though the tempest loudly roars,
> I hear the truth, it liveth.
> And though the darkness round me close,
> Songs in the night it giveth.
>
> No storm can shake my inmost calm,
> When to this rock I'm clinging.
> Since love is Lord of heaven and earth,
> How can I keep from singing.

What is tougher, though, is when the loudly roaring tempest is not so much part of the natural progression of life (as it was for Burt) as it is a brash, blaring affront to it. When a child succumbs to a mysterious illness or a parent to drug addiction, it can be awfully difficult to find the rod and the staff that comfort us through such shadowed valleys. When whole populations, be they neighborhoods, towns, or entire nations, live where fear is as much a part of the fabric of life as the air they breathe or the food they eat, comfort may be more easily sought from a weapon of war than the word of God. Such is the fear in the Middle East now that were Mary and Joseph alive today and had to make their journey from Nazareth to Bethlehem, they would pass through ten Israeli checkpoints, which can only make us wonder how difficult it can be to find God even in the holiest of places.

But find God we do, even in the unholiest of places. The church stands with the oppressed in America's most besieged neighborhoods, the chaplain sits with the disconsolate in pediatric hospitals, and the missionaries build schools in the mud and mire of countries that we have been calling "developing" for over two generations. All the while the prophets call out in righteous indignation to inquire of God and anyone else who will listen why there are still besieged neighborhoods, sick children, and undeveloped nations. As Bill Coffin once said about those whose faith abides even in the most treacherous of circumstances, "like the psalmist, they may pray 'My God, my God, why hast thou forsaken me?' But remember that they begin with 'My God, my God.'" If we can find our way back to God in the most hopeless circumstances, we can find our way when hope is even a faint glimmer in a darkened world.

Coming Back

It is in our nature that we stumble our way into exile just as it is in God's nature that we be called out and given a second chance. Justice is leavened with mercy. But with that second chance we do well to recall the old adage that you cannot step into the same river twice, because having done so once, both you and the river have, however infinitesimally, changed. Life after exile carries the remembrances of life both before and during, which means that when we emerge from it we do so as different people. We know that what we had beforehand is neither our entitlement nor our birthright; with one swing of a hammer it can be lost. Likewise, we know firsthand the pain and alienation that accompany that loss.

Just as Gerry will never forget his years of incarceration, when I escape exile I bring my recollections with me. It is a different river that I step into. What accounts for the difference is the knowledge that though I leave exile it does not leave me, that my acceptance of God's invitation back is a frail thing, that I can allow myself to be distracted, deterred, and derailed. What seduced me once—a lust for power in whatever guise—will always lie in wait.

When I think of this tenuous peace we make with our seducers I recall the last scene from the movie *A Beautiful Mind*, a touching if flawed depiction of how schizophrenia almost destroyed the brilliant mathematician John Nash. For years Nash's illness took the form of paranoid delusions. He had long-standing relationships with three characters who were figments of his imagination: one symbolizing chaste love, another brotherhood, and a third danger. Through arduous therapy Nash regained his mental ballast, and at movie's end he is receiving the Nobel Prize for economics. As he and his family are leaving the award ceremony he looks off across a crowded foyer and sees the three of them standing behind a stanchion. They are just standing there, looking at him. None of them is making any effort to come to him. When his wife asks him if something's wrong, Nash shrugs it off by saying, "No, I just thought I saw an old friend."

The point of this little vignette is that for the good professor, as for all of us, the demons are never far away; at our best we can only keep a roomful of good intentions between us and them. As individuals we will not be rid of them any more than Eve was rid of the temptation that drove her to pluck the fruit in the first place. Collectively, as states and nations and neighborhoods, we will not be rid of them any more than the ancient Israelites were rid of the temptation to worship the gods of materialism, might, or bigotry. Temptations are ours; they are part of our nature and an expression of our free will. They are also reminders that were we to believe in the state of what theologian Paul Tillich called dreamy innocence, where our actions bear neither consequence nor cost, where we look outside ourselves to excuse behaviors that are spawned from within, we would be no less delusional than Nash. As Baudelaire pointed out, we are both the knife and the wound. This is what makes restoration both indispensable and imperfect; it is because every restoration, every second chance, comes with the knowledge that as it is granted we will need a third, and a fourth, and a fifth. Exile is not unfamiliar territory to us, whereas perfection, to paraphrase Paul, is not a thing we can grasp. But restoration is. And when we turn back to God, wounds, warts, and all, we are welcomed. We pledge to God an undying fealty that, try as we might, we will not honor. And God pledges a fealty that will be honored without condition or constraint.

Not of Our Own Design

As much as God seeks to call us back from our self-inflicted exile, it would be theologically dishonest to neglect exile of a different cause. We suffer from the consequences of our own arrogance and insecurity, but we suffer too from the consequences of actions that are not our own. Stray bullets find innocent targets, strange afflictions befall young adults, and financial calamity is visited upon hard-working people who never wanted anything more than to eke out an honest living. Job is no more responsible for his misfortunes than John Nash is for his. There is no satisfying answer to the question of why good people suffer, but we can find comfort in the knowledge that in our suffering, in *all* manner of suffering, restoration is possible. We can find even more comfort in the knowledge that in other people's exiles we can be instruments of healing.

As a colleague of mine is fond of saying, God has no hands but ours, by which he means it is one thing to pray for the poor and quite another to do whatever is in our power and purview to alleviate them of their poverty. Hands made quiet in supplication must also be made busy in restoration. They must be made to dig into our hearts for sympathy and into our pockets for succor. They must wrap themselves around the grieving widow and grab hold of the wayward youth who is slowly slipping away from his family's imperfect love. These hands must curl themselves into fists so as to rail at injustice but also be put to work lessening it. They must applaud the good but also contribute to it. They must be extended in love to our friends and in peace to our enemies. They must be God's hands.

When they are, when they are put to work restoring the broken lives and the broken hearts, *we* are restored, because we cannot simultaneously work for the kingdom and feel exiled from it.

I think of the men and women who so painstakingly restored *La Pietà*, who were able to return her from exile and give her back to the world. Their labors were mighty, their task excruciatingly slow. Each one had to have the touch of a surgeon and the patience of a saint. But more than this, each one had to live with the ambivalent feeling that on the one hand they were bringing lost beauty back to life, but on the other theirs was an imperfect, incomplete work; beauty destroyed by rage is replicated but not duplicated. This is our eternal dilemma: God's perfect love finding us in our most imperfect world.

We are a people of flaws and scars; we know how much God loves us, but we will always be tempted to reach for something beyond the substance of that love. This is *Nostra Pietà*, our pity. It is not just that we welcome God's restorative grace, it is that we need it.

Questions for Discussion

In this chapter I argue that restoration leaves scars. Do you agree, and if so, why are these scars important?

In what ways are Adam and Eve representative of all of us? Why did God put restraints on them in the garden of Eden? What are our forbidden fruits? Our exile?

Think of a metaphorical "exile" that you may have found yourself in. What does the "Eden" look like that is its counterpart, and how can you restore yourself to it?

Chapter 2

Rebirth

Its inhabitants are, as the man once said, "whores, pimps, gamblers, and sons of bitches," by which he meant Everybody. Had the man looked through another peephole he might have said, "Saints and angels and martyrs and holy men," and he would have meant the same thing.

—John Steinbeck

The Troubled Wise Man

"Very truly, I tell you, no one can see the kingdom of God without being born from above" (John 3:3). So says Jesus to the Pharisee Nicodemus in one of the favorite passages of every tent-pitching evangelist of fact or fiction who ever preached a gospel of deliverance from the fiery pits of eternal damnation. Whether it be Elmer Gantry, Aimee McPherson, or Jimmy Swaggart, whether on street corners, tabernacles, or cable TV, with hands flailing and eyes cast pleadingly to the heavens, these preachers of the unadorned word have labored mightily to convince us sinners that this and this alone will save us from those sins. Forthright and plainspoken on the surface, it is only when you dig a little deeper into the story that you discover, in the words of biographer Robert Dalleck, that "history resides in the details." If we want to know what it means to be reborn, or "born from above" (in Greek, *anothen*, which connotes both being born of God and being born again), then those details are worth a closer look.

At his first birth, Nicodemus's parents did what a lot of parents

14

unwittingly do: they saddled him with expectations. His name literally means "conqueror of the people," which, if nothing else, gave the boy a lot to live up to. Whether he conquered anyone is lost to us (although John does refer to him as a "ruler of the Jews"), but what we do know is that he was a scholarly man—he would not have held office as a member of the elite governing body known as the Sanhedrin had he not been—who was schooled in the finer points of Scripture and interpretation. We also know that as a Pharisee (the religious blue bloods of ancient Judaism) his schooling stressed a rigid interpretation of the texts, an unbending respect to the finer points of the Law, and, in all likelihood, a dose of disdain for anyone either less wise or less legalistic (which for many Pharisees was pretty much everyone).

But the erudite Nicodemus, used to answering the questions of others rather than posing questions of his own, is genuinely struck by the work of this uneducated contrarian from the north country. In the dead of night Nicodemus goes to him to ask him about the kingdom of God. When he meets Jesus he does two things. First, in perhaps begrudging recognition of the genius of his teaching, he calls him "rabbi"; and second, in recognition that there is something indeed special about this man, he mentions "these signs [miracles] that you do" (3:2). In other words, the wise, wealthy, and worldly "conqueror of the people" comes before Jesus in a role he is not all that familiar with—a humbled supplicant.

For all the topics that could have come up between the two men, why this one? Why was entry into the kingdom of God so important to the Jews of Jesus' time? It is quite possible that what made it important was that the kingdom represented a kind of celestial rescue from the miseries of the current age. Like all people of all eras who toil under the heavy hand of another, the Jews suffered a sorry fate under the Romans and wanted to believe that freedom was not only something worth believing in, but that it was imminent. The way the American slave spirituals of the nineteenth century spoke of a day when "Babylon's fallin' to rise no more" to usher in "a better world by and by," the Israelites wanted to know how much better, in what ways better, and, most important, what they had to do to gain entry. It was the great and grating mystery that surely burned in the hearts of Nicodemus and his compatriots.

But for all his deference, Nicodemus finds Jesus' answer impenetrable because he fails to hear it as a metaphor. Even when Jesus parses it for him, explaining that it is a birth "of water and Spirit," perhaps even echoing the words of Ezekiel with which the old Pharisee would have been familiar—"I will sprinkle clean water upon you and . . . from all your idols I will cleanse you" (Ezek. 36:25)—we are still not given to believe he ever fully understood what Jesus was getting at. If when he leaves Jesus he is satisfied with what he has heard, the text does not show it.

In this way Nicodemus ceases to be a person and becomes himself a metaphor, becomes every person, becomes all of us, seekers in the darkness, spiritual wanderers in the dead of night. We are the ones unable to see that when Jesus is talking about a new birth he is telling us that before any rank is imposed on us here on earth, before we are defined by the family from which we come, the accolades bestowed on us or the criticisms besetting us, we are children of God. To be born again is to know our very essence, stripped of all the accoutrements that attach to us over time, and in knowing, to become what theologian Paul Tillich called "a new being." It is to take heed of the words of the poet John Webster: "vain the ambition of kings who seek by trophies and dead things to leave a living name behind, and weave but nets to catch the wind." To be born again is to be as unencumbered as that wind.

The Naked Self

For us to rediscover that essence, that fundamental, irreducible core of our being, we must dig beneath the surface assumptions we normally use to define ourselves, and this may have been what Jesus was telling his inquisitor. To be reborn means to put aside old categories that we have accumulated like merit badges and used to sum up lives thus far lived. The core being is deeper than what we do for a living, where we worship, or our political affiliation. It is deeper than our status as a parent, a child, or a spouse, a resident of this or that neighborhood, a member of this or that tribe. It is not a matter of what club would or would not have us as a member, or what university we attended. While any of these or a host of other descriptions might begin to point to who we are, none of them takes us there; they are as accurate as they are inadequate.

Nor is it enough to dig deeper in search of the logic behind our actions and choices, the roots of our will. The decisions we make, the moral code we struggle to live by, the experiences we gather, the expediencies we take and the corners we cut, the self-interests we display, as well as our own fundamental strengths and weaknesses all add hue to the picture of who we are, but still fail to define our essential being—as do our intellect, the compendium of our knowledge, the process of our thoughts, our capacity for reason, the limits of our wisdom, and the depths of our emotions. All of this precedes, informs, and shapes our will, which in turn gives rise to our actions, but even this does not go deep enough, because it does not account for our inherent need to search for meaning in our lives, to perceive the transcendent, to define for ourselves a purpose that is itself part of a larger purpose.

What makes us who we are? *It is our desire for meaning* that we can attach to our lives. When Jesus tells Nicodemus he must be born again, I believe he is telling him that he must reclaim his confession that he is first and foremost not a Pharisee or a governor or a scholar or a good Jew or a good man. He is not first a moral individual or a provider for his family. He is not first a thinking or feeling or even a caring person. He is, before all else, a child loved by God, in whose love he is grounded and therefore from whose love all else—all thoughts and feelings and words and deeds—must originate. Centuries later the great artist Marc Chagall would put it this way: "In our life there is a single color, as on an artist's palette, which provides the meaning of life and art. It is the color of love."

Rebirth is not so much a moment as a mind-set. It is the recognition of who we are by virtue of whose we are. We are children of a God who cares for us, believes in us, and sustains us. As the psalmist entreated his God, "You desire truth in the inward being; therefore teach me wisdom in my secret heart" (Ps. 51:6). It is our desire to live lives of meaning, and it is God's desire that we understand that the most meaningful of lives are those lived in faithful reflection of his love for us.

But just the fact that the psalmist—a man of faith—has to ask this of God, or that Nicodemus, also a man of faith, has to be summoned back to it, indicates that it is a mind-set as uneasily grasped as it is easily forgotten. We want to hold tight to the assurance that we are all made in God's image, and we want that assurance to be the very underpinning of our thoughts and feelings, our words and deeds, our motivations and dreams. But it is easily lost when the image becomes blurred or veiled, all but undetectable to all but the most discerning eye.

This is why when I recognize the richness of my life, when the people who mean the most to me are safe and well cared for, and when I want for nothing of any real substance, it is easy for me to echo the words of Keats, "Wherein lies happiness? In that which becks our ready minds to fellowship divine, a fellowship with essence." For God's love is so close and so in evidence at such a moment that I can believe myself to be anchored in it for all my days both before and hence. Past times of trouble are forgotten or minimized. Occasions of spiritual doubt or moral lassitude are self-edited out of my history, because it is a new day. I am born again. I know that God walks with me. I know that I am God's. And I know as well that everything around me, seen and unseen, is also God's. I feel a profound sense of peace and gratitude, the way a newborn might feel such utter contentment when he is swathed and held by a loving adult whose warm, caressing arms reassure him, "I am here with you, and everything is alright."

The Wounded Self in a Fallen World

But what about when all isn't alright? "The earth is the LORD's and all that is in it," said David (Ps. 24:1), but that does not mean all is well on it or that I cannot lose my way in it. There are times when such unspeakable sadness enters our lives, when kind people are arbitrarily hurt, or financial calamity besets a good family already living on the edge of ruin, that the voice of God is drowned by the din of sorrow. Robert Heilbroner, the founder of Bread for the World, tells of an Iranian peasant who literally lost his sight because he could not afford the $4 he mistakenly thought he needed for entry into a hospital where he could have been cured. How will this man find the way to his core when he can no longer find his way home?

I grew up in a town where the kids were no more gentle or cruel to one another than in most other towns. There were always kids who were not invited to parties because they did not dress right, did not look right, or were not handsome enough. When there was a pickup ball game others (or maybe they were the same kids) were not chosen because they were not skilled enough. Now, as an adult, I have to wonder, with each childhood broken heart (and how frequently children break one another's hearts) how hard was it for those young people to find meaning deep within their souls when they felt their bodies had so betrayed them.

Nor is alienation the provenance just of the downtrodden and the brokenhearted. It also lies just beneath the cool exterior of the bullies who are their tormentors, the ones who wear their arrogance like a fig leaf over their insecurities, who delight in building themselves up by tearing others down, and who believe that waiting at the back of the line, obeying speed limits, or paying full price for anything is for chumps. God's love is foreign to them as well, not because of an immensity of shame but because of a paucity of compassion, which Eric Hoffer said was "the one thing that stands apart from the continuous traffic between good and evil proceeding within us."

Our Lonely Search

The impediments to an inner search for God are not always a matter of how we treat or are treated by others. Sometimes it is simply a matter of how we treat ourselves. Americans are not predisposed to prolonged soul searching. As the playwright Eric Bentley once put it, "instead of language we have jargon; instead of principles, slogans; and instead of genuine ideas, bright suggestions." The search for meaning can be long and lonely.

It is long because to get there we have to have the courage to give less weight to the sorts of things that have long given us value—our status, our things, our popularity. They are things that culture has outfitted us with, but while some of them may win us praise among our peers, they have no ultimate meaning before God. So we lighten our load, leaving them behind. It is lonely because surrendering, even temporarily, the things we have spent our lifetimes acquiring separates us from the people around us who also depend on those things to define their identity and worth.

My favorite description of the search comes from Sister Mary Louise, a steely little Harley-driving woman with bright eyes, a gentle smile, and the toughness of a stevedore. Jailed periodically for civil disobedience, she especially enjoyed what she called "the subversive activity of leading my fellow inmates in hymn sings" because it drove the guards crazy. Sister Mary's vocation was itself one of self-abnegation, but as she once said to me, "Mine is a humbling profession, and that's good. The problem is that I'm proud to be humble. When I take a journey of rebirth the pride's the first thing that has to go."

"The journey is like a trip through a labyrinth," she said, referring to the winding maze religious seekers prayerfully walk that draws you to its core, and then leads you out again. "With each step toward the center, I can feel myself shedding the baggage I carry day to day. Preoccupations slowly slip by the wayside, and I become more conscious of God. In time my consciousness of God eclipses everything else. As I get near the center I begin to feel its tug, and when I arrive there I have a profound feeling of cleansing and purification. My sins are gone. My anxieties are gone. My identity as a nun, or an aunt, or an Orioles fan, or an ex-con, are all gone. It's just me with God. I never expect to weep when I get there, but I always do. My tears are my baptism, all over again."

But there is more, because the core is only the halfway point. "I wish that I could stay there forever," she tells me, "but just because it's the core of my being doesn't mean it's my earthly home. So after a time, I must leave and begin the slow and winding journey out again.

"This is a process, too, and it allows me to reenter the world with a new consciousness of myself as a child of God, born anew. This consciousness not only warms my heart but compels me to carry that warmth to whatever cold places God calls me to. My rebirth gives me both a deeply personal sense of intimacy with God and a profound commitment to social justice. The healing that I experience at the center of the labyrinth reaffirms my faith, just as my carrying it out to people who are wounded and places that are broken reaffirms my vocation. It doesn't do any good to experience birth—the first time or later times—if you're not then going to experience life."

Sister Mary hit upon a tension that divides the faithful in this country. Many of us are content to luxuriate in God's love without a thought to what that means for our responsibility to the greater world, while others, in their determination to bring a prophetic voice to that world, dismiss the "born-again" experience by ceding it to a bunch of unsophisticated religious hysterics and their lemming-like followers.

Neither is sufficient, of course, and neither is fair. When we receive the healing power of God's love but fail to apply it to a bleeding world, it is as though we have stumbled upon the empty tomb of Christ crucified, heard the good news that we are forgiven our sins, and then turned a deaf ear to the chamber's echo, "Now, go to Galilee" (Matt. 28:10). Faith without works, as James pointed out, is dead (Jas. 2:16, 26). But the reverse is true too, for if we do the works without the faith, tend to others' bodies without replenishing our own souls, we risk paying either homage or lip service to an irrelevant God who is nothing more than an appendage to the good works by which we define ourselves and for which we congratulate ourselves.

But faith and works together are a formidable force. When we are reborn, when we reconvene with the God who sanctifies our life, we are reminded that this God sanctifies all life, that there is no room for arrogance or superiority, and that whatever work we do on earth is not for the glorification of our will but for the fulfillment of God's.

It is hard won, this recognition, because it means loving as God loves. It means loving the small-minded bigot and the small-hearted miser. It means loving the impatient neighbor who throws a fit when a child's errant softball lands in her yard, and wishing only good things for an old friend who has betrayed your trust. It also means caring for the welfare of those whose deeds we truly loathe and assiduously oppose—the politician whose ambition has bested her pledge to serve, the misogynist who enjoys demeaning women. Remember that while Jesus implored us to love our enemies, he did not tell us not to make any. To live as though we have been born again is to love even what we are determined to change because we know that God dwells and stirs in all of us.

This is why Jesus answered Nicodemus's question the way he did. The old lawmaker wanted to know how to gain entry into the kingdom, and Jesus answered by telling him to forget his laws and remember his soul, for that is where he would find his way. He was telling Nicodemus to find the love of God where God first put it, within him, and to project that love into a world that is not ready for it. This is the kingdom, Jesus was telling him. It is found in the life of the contrarian who, forced to choose between allegiance to Caesar and allegiance to God, will choose God not hesitantly but gladly, and will just as gladly bear the burden that Caesar exacts. It is the world where people walk two miles with a stranger when the law tells them to walk one, where a beggar who asks for a shirt is given a coat, and where a cheek slapped in anger is turned in mercy.

When I think of the kingdom of God, Geoffrey Canada comes to mind. Canada is a charismatic community organizer who works with at-risk children in Harlem. His passion centers around ensuring that these children get decent educations, and he moves heaven and earth to see to it that they do not stumble over the kinds of impediments that more affluent children never face. When someone observed, "So what you want to do is help these kids overcome the odds," Canada replied pointedly but graciously, "Ultimately, no. What I want to do is *change* the odds. What I want to do is *even* the odds." That is the kingdom: not pity—equality.

The kingdom is all this and more because it is the one place where we recognize to the very depths of our being that no power that can divide us is as great as the one power that can unite us. It is a kingdom that is already there if only we will live it. That is why Jesus' exact words to Nicodemus were that by being born again he would "*see* the kingdom."

To Be Born Again, and Again

When people talk about conversion experiences I think less of a drop-to-your-knees, lightning-bolt moment of heavenly clarity than about a recurring choice that presents itself at every turn—however momentous or quotidian—of every day. In each instance we choose to believe either that God is in our hearts or he is not, and the content of that choice reveals the texture of our faith. The child of God, born anew, embodies Paul's well-worn words to the Corinthians of a love that is patient and kind, not jealous or boastful, not arrogant or rude; a love that does not insist on its own way, and does not rejoice in wrong; a love that bears all things, hopes all things, and endures all things (1 Cor. 13:4–7).

When we hold firm to this belief we demonstrate it in our loving actions, just as when we demonstrate loving actions they make firm our belief. Even at day's end we muster the strength to help our children, not because it is the easy recourse but because it is the faithful one, and in choosing faith over ease, God over Caesar, we are (at least in that moment) born again, living in the kingdom. Love is patient and kind.

We listen to those with whom we do not agree because we are willing to accept that even someone we do not like can teach us something, even if what they teach us is the limits of our tolerance and the danger of our biases. Love is not arrogant and does not insist on its own way.

When illness befalls someone we care about, or ourselves, or when bad news comes from unexpected places and our world wobbles, we still return to warm ourselves by the embers of God's love. When a relationship falls apart or when we are told with staged sincerity that we were the second-best candidate for the job, we still cling to God because love bears all things, hopes all things, and endures all things.

I do not believe, as the old James Lowell hymn has it, that "once in every life and nation comes a moment to decide." We decide daily, constantly, *religiously*, second chance after second chance after second chance. In each decision we are either accepting God into our hearts or shutting her out, and even saints among us, though they often accept her, sometimes do not. As Steinbeck suggested in *Cannery Row*, we are *all* pimps and gamblers and martyrs and angels. Finally, I believe that acceptance of God means acceptance of ourselves as if we were newly born—not to be lauded for our merits, condemned for our failures, or measured by either. Rather it is to be invigorated by the expansive opportunity to live in accordance with God's challenging, comforting, demanding, enriching, abiding presence, and in each day, the opportunity to get it right.

Perhaps Nicodemus Got It Right

It was risky of Nicodemus to seek Jesus which is why he went out as he did in the dead of night so as not to be caught by his peers, and, for all his wisdom, to confess to Jesus that he did not know where to find the key to the kingdom. It also had to be painful to learn that that kingdom was not first and foremost about an accumulation of good works—for these he had done—but about a stripping away of *all* works, until all that he is left with is himself as a new being, utterly empty, raw before God. As an old man this must have been hard to hear.

But hear it he did, and I suspect he took it to heart, because when even Jesus' friends had begun to abandon him, Nicodemus, in his own cautious way, tried to come to his defense. It happened when the Pharisees were debating what to do with Jesus, and the consensus was that he be arrested, tried, and in all certainty convicted and punished for his sins. Among the Pharisees, only Nicodemus argued for patience and fairness, imploring his colleagues to hear what Jesus had to say in his own defense. "Our law does not judge people without first giving him a hearing to find out what they are doing, does it?" (John 7:51), he asked them, for which they then accused him of being a traitor. They were not particularly bold words, save for the fact that he was the only one who dared to speak them, and any words that cut against an incensed throng can be nothing but bold.

Nicodemus failed to win freedom for the man whose words haunted and held him. But perhaps all was not lost, because our last glimpse of Nicodemus is after Jesus' death, where he and Joseph of Arimathea have taken the body away for proper burial. He did not have to do this, but he chose to. Perhaps it was an act of obedience, but I like to think it was one of gratitude. Imagine this: he takes the body into his arms the way a parent might a newborn. He quietly rubs it with cleansing oils, swaddles it in cloths, and gently lays it down to sleep. It is not the sleep of death, he knows, but of birth. For this Son of God has died the death of the body but will live again. For no matter how hard we try to kill the promise of the kingdom, it is in our hearts, where no amount of evil can ever hope to destroy it. This Nicodemus believes, and with this belief, he too is born again.

Questions for Discussion

What does it mean to be "born again," and what is its relationship to "the kingdom"? Should we understand the kingdom today the same way it was understood when Jesus spoke of it?

What do we have to give up in order to be born again? What problems might this pose?

Is rebirth a one-time-only religious moment, a moment of conversion, or do we have the opportunity for "rebirths" throughout our lives?

What are the impediments you face in your inner search for God?

What are the social justice implications of being born again?

Chapter 3

Reconciliation

*Only the brave know how to forgive. . . . A coward never for-
gave; it is not in his nature.*

—Lawrence Sterne

Abraham Lincoln once said of George McClellan that the general
must put a high value on truth because he used it so sparingly. God
might have said the same thing about Jacob; in fact, Jacob makes
McClellan look like a Cub Scout. I have mixed feelings about Jacob,
nonetheless. On the one hand, he is a poster boy for dishonest behavior and its consequences; on the other, in his moment of awareness,
when he came face-to-face with himself and all that he had done, he
made his amends. This is why he is an important proxy for all of us,
because he embodies both the supreme weakness and the unique
strength of human character—the capacity for sin and the ability to
atone. At root, all sin is composed, at least in part, of deception
(whether of ourselves or of others), just as all reconciliation is composed of forgiveness.

The Seeds of Deceit

Tradition has it that Jacob and his twin brother, Esau, struggled for
supremacy even before they were born. As the legend goes, Isaac
named his second-born son Jacob (which means "heel") because
when Rebekah was giving birth and Esau was the first to emerge,
Jacob, wanting to accrue all the rights that come with being the first-

born, supposedly grabbed hold of his brother's heel and tried to pull him back. The historicity of this story is of course long lost in the vapors of time, but the implied consequence is what is important, because the firstborn would be the one entitled to inherit Isaac's divine blessing that he himself had inherited from his father, Abraham. Jacob's cunning did not serve him that time, but it did a few years later.

Again, according to legend (and let us remember that not all truths need be historical ones), as a young man Jacob had the unbridled gall to deceive his aged, feeble, addled, and half-blind father in order to receive from him the blessing of the firstborn—Esau's birthright. Jacob wore Esau's clothes, and the old man could not detect the ruse. Thinking it was Esau standing before him, Isaac gave the wily Jacob the blessing that was by all rights his brother's, that God would give him "of the dew of heaven, and of the fatness of the earth" (Gen. 27:28), and "Let peoples serve you, and nations bow down to you" (27:29). When Esau exposed the deception, a crestfallen Isaac had no recourse to right the wrong. What had been done was binding and irrevocable; it could not be undone. So it was that this covenantal cornerstone, the very foundation without which Judaism would not be Judaism nor Christianity Christianity, had been bequeathed to a fraud.

For Esau the wound was deep but not mortal. Healing required a gesture from Jacob that to many probably seemed impossible. The brothers had been physically and emotionally separated from each other for many years. On the eve of their meeting, Jacob took measure of what had to this point been a life largely driven by deceits, and atoned, at one point crying to God that he was "not worthy of the least of all the steadfast love" (32:10) that God had shown him. Few would have disagreed.

Then, after setting aside a generous peace offering for his brother, Jacob entered into a mysterious wrestling match from dark until dawn with an angel who wounded but also blessed him by bestowing a new name on him. The purpose of this drama was to make Jacob—now named Israel, or "striven with God"—understand that favor in God's eyes was gained not through sleight of hand but by change of heart, by facing life honestly, wrestling with our demons, perhaps suffering at their hands, persevering to the point of exhaustion and beyond, and even bearing proudly the cuts and wounds endured by that perseverance. Indeed, when he has finished with the angel we see him dog-tired, limping, but toward a rising sun—pain and hope, the bookends of life. He was now prepared to make his amends with his brother. Reconciliation—literally, "friendship again"—could now happen.

What completed the healing was the munificence with which Esau greeted his chastened brother, for what could have been the battlefield on which Esau extracted his just revenge became instead a place where mercy bested hatred. Instead of drawing their swords the two men opened their arms, embraced, kissed, and wept the bittersweet, soft, cleansing tears of contrition and mercy. While it is not recorded in Scripture, I have to believe that they stayed a while, shared a meal, and reminisced about the better moments of their childhood. Youthful games were called to mind, as well as pranks played on other kids. They remembered the scary stories they would tell each other deep into the night when their parents were sure they were asleep, and the silly, simple games they would devise to keep away the boredom when working in the fields. They did this all because they were brothers, and because memory can be sifted when the occasion calls for it, so that if what we seek are its golden nuggets, that is what we will find. As Shakespeare wrote in *Macbeth*, "I cannot but remember such things were, that were most precious to me."

Though from here they went their separate ways and would not see each other again until years later when they laid their father to rest, they were now more intimately bound than even when they first shared their mother's womb. Such is the power of atonement and the gift of forgiveness, humility and generosity entwined in divine partnership. Like twin boys who are different to their very core yet dependent upon one another, neither is complete without his counterpart.

It is that entwining that is so important, and that is axiomatic for all of us, because we have no choice but to be in relationship with one another. Not only is it fundamental to how we have come to survive on earth, it is fundamental to our nature; it is something we cannot *not* do. Insofar as what we do affects others and what others do affects us, our lives are veritable webs of relationships. We exist in relationship to those we know but also to those we do not, to our friends and to our enemies, with people we see every day of our lives and do not think twice about, people we love with a depth we cannot fathom, and people we will go lifelong never having met.

But if relationship is a mandate, it is one without guarantee. That is, when we hold together, one to another, it is not certainty that binds us so much as it is trust. In the deep of the evening on a long, deserted street, I cannot know that the strangers walking toward me mean me no harm any more than they can know that I mean them none. When we vote for a candidate, buy goods from a grocer, or assure our child that there are no monsters under the bed, we are forging a bond based not on inviolate guarantees but on pledges whose durability can but be hoped for with trust as yet unearned. Only time will tell if, as the poet Francois Malherbe wrote, "the fruits will outdo what the flowers have promised."

But when the flowers have promised what the fruits fail to deliver, or when the monsters rise from beneath the bed, what then of trust? What happens when young people suffer because a priest or a president fails to keep them out of harm's way, or old people suffer because their children, who were once so quick to receive their love, are now so slow to return it? What happens when a brother steals the blessing of another brother? How do we forgive what we cannot, and must not, forget?

Whence Forgiveness?

Had Jacob and Esau done battle that day it would not have been the first time blood was shed in the name of God, nor, of course, would it have been the last. The one thing as maddening as humankind's penchant for war is our willingness to sanctify it with the language of faith. Yet even in today's war-scorched landscape of the Holy Land, there is hope, a vestige of which can be found not fifty miles from where Jacob wrestled with his angel. Here, in the tiny Israeli town of Ramat-Efal, an unlikely alliance of Palestinians and Israelis are wrestling with theirs. In the name of God and through the fog of war, it is broken trust they know all too well, and it is reconciliation that they seek.

They go by the name "Parents' Circle," and are all bereaved people who have lost family members to the Israeli-Palestinian conflict. Together they support peace, reconciliation, and tolerance as the only way to achieve a just resolution to the conflict that has raged for over fifty years and claimed countless innocent lives. One of their more eloquent members is a salt-and-pepper-haired woman by the name of Robi Damelin, an Israeli in her sixties who refers to herself as "an ancient woman who's still learning" and whose austerity of dress cannot hide her elegance and grace. Robi's son, David, was serving in the Israeli military when he was killed by a Palestinian sniper, and she grieves his loss every day. Her journey has not been easy; it never is when a parent has to bury a child, especially one who has been felled by needless violence. But the circle has had what she refers to as a cleansing effect on her. It has shown her, she says, that there is no such thing as "Palestinian pain" or "Israeli pain," only human pain, and the sharing of it among themselves—talking, listening, understanding, forgiving—provides a powerful bond between these two communities that have long believed they had nothing in common beyond contempt for one another.

For Palestinian Ali Abu Awaad membership in the circle came in a different manner but landed him in the same pool of pain. Awaad was in Saudi Arabia receiving medical treatment after having been shot during the Intifada when word came that his brother had been killed by an Israeli soldier. He believes deeply that the Palestinians are right in wanting a homeland, and his immediate reaction could have been to continue the struggle in his brother's name. But he realizes that this line of thinking is futile. One of his observations about the difficulty of warring factions to reconcile with one another is that "people are too busy thinking they are right. Everybody thinks they are right and the other guy is wrong. In the circle we don't ask you to be right. We ask you to be honest." Indeed, when I had the opportunity to hear Awaad and Damelin speak of their common circumstances, I heard no competing claims to a moral high ground, only conciliatory words about the need for all human beings to lay down their swords and shields and study war no more (as the venerable hymn puts it).

Their point is that if healing is to come between warring groups, everyone concerned must look deep within and ask themselves what they can do to make for a just peace. For Awaad and Damelin, as emblematic of all Israelis and Palestinians, as emblematic of any people caught in the snares of intractable conflict—be they soldiers on a battlefield or kids on a playing field—what this means is having the courage to put a higher price on pure peace than on a flawed sense of justice.

By peace I do not mean a coward's capitulation to the tyranny of the enemy. What I do mean is letting go of, in Awaad's words, the need to be *right*. Here is an example that does not carry the drama of war but makes the point nonetheless. Sharon and Nick had been married fourteen years when Nick finally came clean about how his secret passion for gambling had brought them to the brink of financial ruin. Beyond losing the family savings, his habit had cost him his job, on top of which he owed some very unsavory people large sums of money.

Thanks to some saintly generosity on the part of Sharon's parents, they were able to save the house (and Nick's kneecaps) and set themselves on a long and arduous path toward financial reclamation. But some deep damage had been done because of Nick's violation of Sharon's trust. When they first came for counseling (the modest price her parents exacted for their generosity), an awful lot of emotional bloodletting went on. But in time Nick, who initially tried to finesse away or at the very least minimize his failings, summoned up the courage to admit them, acknowledge the wreckage they had brought to his family, accept sole responsibility for them, and ask only that Sharon consider forgiving him. Later still—*much* later—Sharon, as she put it, "dragged myself kicking and screaming to the altar of forgiveness. But I finally relented."

The experience was a costly but healthy exercise for them. It forced Nick to confront his sickness and become accountable for his actions, but it also taught Sharon that he was deserving not only of her anger but of her compassion. Their relationship matured as naiveté surrendered to the realization of the hard work of marriage. They had frank, difficult conversations, and trust, because it was now harder to earn, was more cherished.

What Sharon and Nick went through mirrors the historic give-and-take that occurred between Jacob and Esau. In both cases, trust was shattered in the face of deception and personal gain. Both Sharon and

Esau were within their rights to punish those who had deceived them, and it was both Nick's confession and Jacob's that allowed mercy to soften justice. In both instances self-examination yielded humility, open and honest conversation soothed hostilities, and out of the struggle, a new day dawned. As Ali Abu Awaad might have put it, it dawned because two people saw that it was more important to be honest than right.

The Paradox That Is Our Nature: We Love the Good, and the Bad

So what is it that tethers us to our baser impulses when reconciliation seems to beckon us heavenward, to our loftier ones? Why are we bewitched by the idea of healing old wounds but bewildered by how to accomplish it? I believe there are two internal forces that do battle with our better instincts. Neither one is insurmountable, but both are formidable. The first is the drive to avenge a wrong done to us; the second is a sense of self-righteousness that comes with feeling victimized.

Lord Byron was ahead of his time when he made the observation in *Don Juan* that revenge is sweet, because years later researchers determined that our brains are in fact biologically wired to satisfy the need for vengeance the same way, and in the same location (the prefrontal cortex, to be precise) they are wired to satisfy our need for food. We literally hunger for it. Unfortunately, it is a kind of junk-food hunger: the satisfaction is fleeting, addictive, and unhealthy.

This is why the families of murder victims so often report an odd feeling of hollowness when the murderer himself is incarcerated or executed by the state. As Frank Lucianna, a criminal attorney with over fifty years' practice under his belt, told me, "the punishment becomes a symbol of their desire for vengeance, but when it is carried out they are still left with an overriding sense of loss, and what 'sweetness' they may have anticipated is scant and cheap. It dissipates in a hurry and can leave them even more torn up inside because they have asked too much of it; what they thought would lighten their pain has only left them with further disappointment."

The second obstacle is the belief that we are right and our adversary is wrong. Giving that up either as myth (more often than not nobody's entirely blameless) or just in terms of the moral power you think it holds (Esau *was* right, but in and of itself what did that solve?) is not something we do willingly or instinctively. This was in part why Sharon had to be "dragged kicking and screaming" to forgive Nick; she enjoyed holding the high ground and was afraid that by letting him off that hook she would also be letting herself off that perch, from where she enjoyed a view of moral superiority that she would not relinquish gladly.

The Paradox That Is Our Salvation: Strength in Surrender

It takes an enormous amount of strength to descend a perch, sheathe a sword, or unclench a fist. We do not want to put ourselves in a position of vulnerability, either through admitting our wrongs or forgiving those of others, because we do not know—will not trust—what the other person will do with our gesture. They become our monsters under the bed. But we do well here to remember that acts are courageous precisely because we do not know their outcome, and that trust demands uncertainty no less than uncertainty demands trust. Jacob could not know how Esau would receive his humility any more than Esau could know how Jacob would receive his generosity.

But even when trusts have been violated, we have no choice but to take the risk—if timidly and with reservations—which, in its purest form, is the risk of surrender. Only by going out on a limb, where the tree is weakest and our footing least sure, do we get to the good fruit. For Jacob the first step of surrender was confession, which he made when he relinquished any pretense he might have harbored that the theft of his brother's blessing was justified ("I am not worthy of the least of all the steadfast love and faithfulness that you have shown to your servant," Gen. 32:10).

The second step was atonement, which he made when he surrendered his riches as rough compensation for the weight of his sins ("from what he had with him he took a present for his brother Esau, two hundred female goats and twenty male goats, two hundred ewes

and twenty rams, . . ." Gen. 32:13–14). For Esau, it was through forgiveness that he surrendered his claim to moral supremacy and the
righteousness of his indignation, and with it the crippling, consuming
anger he carried with him for all those years ("Esau ran to meet him,
and embraced him, and fell on his neck and kissed him, and they
wept," 33:4). For both, it meant turning their relationship on its head
by relying on trust to redefine a brotherhood that had heretofore been
defined by deceit, no small order. For all of us it is perhaps like the
disciple Peter stepping out of the boat and into that stormy sea at the
beckoning of his Lord; it is the tentative embrace of an uncertain
future that we take armed only with hope that a friendship once lost
can be found again.

But that is no meager armament, because it means that in our over-
tures we are replacing our cards, not just tossing them in. In Jacob's
confession he surrendered the fiction of his entitlement and received
in its place a lighter heart and a cleansed conscience. When Esau surrendered his anger he gained the capacity to love his only brother
without hindrance or obstacle and be loved in return. Surrender is not
an act of morbid martyrdom; it is the product of a wisdom that directs
us to choose what we need over what we want and in so doing dis-
poses us to the possibility of reconciliation.

So perhaps reconciliation finally comes down to this question: Is
one person capable of making an overture of sacrifice, and is another
capable of responding in kind? Can the illusion of power be replaced
by the authenticity of love? Think again of Robi Damelin and Ali Abu
Awaad and the countless others like them who, having already seen
their own loved ones sacrificed to hatred, surrendered their desire to
exact an eye for an eye, and put in its place humility leavened with
the recognition that in that hatred there is all heat and no light. Their
gesture is both virtuous and wise and therefore worthy in and of itself,
but we are remiss if we do not ask whether anyone else will listen to
them and heed their example. Will the provocateurs of war continue
to transform fears and resentments into bullets and bombs? Or might
modest gatherings such as the Parents' Circle represent the first seeds
of a movement that will bring a homeland to dispossessed Palestinians and secure borders to embattled Israelis? If so, might the flaming
madness of other wars be slowly doused as well?

When my heart and mind turn closer to home I think of the extraordinary witness of the Amish community in Nickel Mines, Pennsylvania, where on a warm October afternoon in 2006 a man by the name of Carl Roberts entered their little one-room schoolhouse and executed five of their children before turning the gun on himself. But despite all the evil that filled the room that afternoon, there was space for Christ as well, whose love was in the hearts of all those children but channeled through one in particular, a thirteen-year-old girl named Marian Fisher. Marian was the oldest child in the school that day and begged Roberts to kill her first because she believed that if he did this he would spare the younger ones. The nobility she displayed just moments from her own death was later mirrored by the wider community. Only hours after the event left them deep in shock and alone with their sadness, members of this community went to Roberts's home not to rail against his madness and the suffering it had visited upon them nor to seek a blood measure of revenge from his kin. They went to his family, and they sat, and prayed, and cried with them. And they told them that as difficult as it was to bear this great burden, there was forgiveness in their hearts.

Because it is the unfamiliar as opposed to the commonplace that captures our attention, it was not the grotesquery of Roberts's actions but the gentility of the Amish response that made us linger around this story. The air was full of paeans to these "simple people" and their "simple faith." We admired them. But it is admiration at arm's length, the way a young boy admires his favorite baseball player because the player can do things that the boy believes he himself will always be incapable of. So there are still two hundred million guns on our streets, while tortured souls like Roberts still receive our scorn instead of our pity. The grace we saw exhibited by these people whose faith is simple only because they do not complicate it with equivocations remains a thing we are quicker to revere than replicate.

But even if the boy will never play like his hero, we should encourage him to try. Let us not be discouraged when our own sense of kindness pales beside the luminescence of these good people. Instead, let us be compelled by it, let us aspire to a goodness so pure that we may never attain it but in the very act of reaching for it will make ourselves better people. In a spirit of reconciliation let us forgive old hurts and forget new slights. Let us work a little harder at those relationships that do require hard work but not take for granted those that do not. Perhaps there is a letter to an estranged sibling that is long overdue, or a friendship that is slowly dying because an apology is lodged in the throat and will not come easily. Perhaps there is a relationship so frayed that it is beyond repair, but at least we can free ourselves of the poisoning anger we still harbor toward this person who is as sure that we have wronged her as we are that she has wronged us. When salvation is still barely within reach, perhaps there is some humility that must be gained before the friendship is lost, but this is not a bad thing because, lest we forget, the word *humility* comes from the same root as the word *human*: both derive from *humus*, meaning "to be of the earth." To err is human. To forgive is too. As Paul put it, "Do not be conformed to this world, but be *trans*formed" (Rom. 12:2).

Jacob and Esau were two men who came of age in a warrior culture, and whose love for one another had been sorely tested. In a world where differences of great magnitude were most often settled by the shedding of blood, they had staked out what was to be their field of battle. But in the end, as the sun rose and brother came out to meet brother, they were not conformed to that world, they were transformed, as was the place itself, the very earth beneath them. The *humus*, the stuff of humanity and humility, was not desecrated by their blood, but consecrated by their tears. For this is what happens when people reconcile. They make holy again a place that for too long was absent the forgiving love of God.

Questions for Discussion

Do you agree or disagree with the statement, "At root, all sin is composed, at least in part, of deception"?

What are some of the steps we must take to atone for our sins?

Is it possible to forgive others and still hold them accountable for their misdeeds?

Can concepts like atonement, forgiveness, and reconciliation be applied to national and international issues? How?

How is forgiveness a liberating experience?

Chapter 4

Remembrance

> *Abruptly the poker of memory stirs the ashes of recollection
> and uncovers a forgotten ember, still smoldering down there,
> still hot, still glowing, still red as red.*
> —William Manchester

You Must Remember This

It is one thing to anticipate a feeling—sort of the way we anticipate
the end of a joke—but quite another to be hijacked by an unexpected
emotion. Feelings that lie in wait for us, sneak up, and jump out at us
as if from nowhere are the ones that really grab us. Their power is
often somehow connected to an old memory, a moment in our past
that we are either able to recall or unable to suppress.

This is what happened to my friend Caroline, and it left her breathless. She was hijacked by a surprised feeling born of remembrance. It
had been about three months since Max, Caroline's husband of forty-
six years, had died suddenly in the night. But by now the holidays were
over, his birthday had come and gone, and she had survived—though
she did not know how—their wedding anniversary. Now, she decided,
it was time to start packing his things and giving them away.

"I was doing alright," she told me, "I really was. Until I got to this
one pair of cufflinks. Pearl cufflinks. Silver trimming. A little chip
taken out of the corner of one of them. I don't know what it was about
them, but when I picked them up, and ran them through my fingers, I
just lost it. I sat down on the bed, and I wept, and I wept."

Perhaps it was their beauty, or perhaps they triggered some distant memory of an evening years ago when they themselves were beautiful, an elegant dinner perhaps, a whisk across the dance floor, a night of lovemaking and love taking. Or perhaps it was simply that they were apt symbols, reminders of this man to whom she linked herself until death would part them, as death did.

For whatever reason, these cufflinks became her totem, her touchstone, the object that, in this very private moment, served as a blunt reminder of what she had had, and what she had lost, of a man with whom she shared memories and who must now become part of her past, a memory himself. As Robert Frost wrote in *To Earthward,* "Of tears, the aftermark / Of almost too much love / The sweet of bitter bark / And burning clove."

This is what it means to remember. In memory we relive our events and our experiences, the bliss and the pain, the tedium and the excitement, the delights and the disappointments that are our own personal history. Without it we would have no sense of connection, either to our past or to the others who are an indispensable part of that past. With it, though, we are rooted, joined to others and to *their* histories by common stories.

We learn from these stories (ours and others), take solace in them, are sometimes inspired by them, and other times hurt by them. But in all of them we are reminded that this is what it means to be alive, to be uniquely who we are. Our lives are part of a continuum that began on the day of our birth, and, in community, that continuum stretches as far back as that inimitable moment when God first breathed life into being and deemed it good. It is an ongoing story, as are we.

For Caroline the memory she recalled stung, but that does not negate its worth: better that she meet Max's death with grief than indifference. Over time, if she grieves well, the pain will slowly be eclipsed by a sense of gratitude that she could have had such love in her life. For all the heartache his memory engenders now, I do not believe God wants her to forget him, because there is nothing to gain by forgetting.

Indeed, just as memory is an indispensable part of who we are, in God's eyes it is even more. It is a mandate. Our history is sacred.

We *must* remember. When, in the book of Chronicles, for instance, in the reign of David, the ark of the covenant is brought into Jerusalem, and David says to the gathered priests, "Remember the wonderful works [God] has done, his miracles, and the judgments he uttered" (1 Chr. 16:12), David is not speaking just to them but also to us about a God of judgment and salvation. Likewise, when the thief on the cross asks Jesus to "remember me when you come into your kingdom" (Luke 23:42), it is now meant for *our* ears, that we might remember the liberation of one dying man that was brought about by another dying man.

Our sacred texts are not intended to relegate these moments to the past but to preserve them for all generations, that we might literally re-member them to reassemble the various parts into a coherent whole. This is why Ezekiel tells the ancient Hebrews: "They shall live in the land . . . in which your ancestors lived; *they and their children and their children's children*" (Ezek. 37:25), because *we* are their children's children. The history embedded in the Bible is *our* history. We are accountable to the same God, subject to the same scrutiny, heirs to the same covenant, stewards of the same land.

Memory and Compassion

Remember; remembrance; memory; memorial. The concept appears over two hundred times in our Scriptures and is there not only to lodge a distant thought or event in our minds but to stir in us, teach us, chastise us, and promise us. What we are called on to remember is informative, but it is more. It is inspiring, humbling, thoughtful, evocative, and sometimes even *pro*vocative.

Think of the scene in the first chapters of the book of Deuteronomy, where, after forty years of wandering, forty years of danger, doubt, peril, and privation, the triumphant Hebrews are on the verge of entering the promised land. Moses, their spiritual leader, who has led them this far, who for those forty years has inspired them never to give up, will not be going with them. But in his last address to them he does not play to that sense of triumphalism. Once more, he teaches them, reminding them that humility (perhaps at this moment in short supply) must always be a bedrock of their identity.

As the crowd stands eager to put the hardships of their past behind them and to reap the benefits of this long-deferred and well-earned promise, Moses sends them off by telling them if there is one thing they must bring with them into this new land it is the memory of their old one. "Remember," he tells them, "that *you were a slave in the land of Egypt*, and the LORD your God brought you out from there with a mighty hand and an outstretched arm" (Deut. 5:15).

What Moses is telling them is twofold: First, never forget that your God is a God of freedom; though this was the first time you needed deliverance, he is reminding them, it will not be the last. There will be times when you will need to be delivered from the consequences of your sins, the exhaustion of your spirits, the darkness of your doubts, or the table of your enemies. When those times come, remember what your God did for you those many years ago.

Second, never forget what it feels like to be enslaved by another, because without this memory you will not understand how precious it is to be a liberated people. He might have added that it is only in remembering your own captivity that you can have compassion for others who are enslaved, be it by the hand of another nation, the grind of poverty, the degradation of racism, or any other burden that might deny a people their freedom. Treat them as if they are your own, he is saying, because where they are, you have been, and may one day return. Such is the nature of compassion; our own memories allow us to feel the pain of another's memories. And such is the nature of memory that the stories of our forebears, and the lessons imparted to them, are our inheritance.

The Sacred in the Secular

The power of memory is more than the power of our sacred texts. When we read a story such as, say, Moses at Canaan, or Ruth at Moab, or the wise men at the manger, the words transport us back to another place and time. But other things work this way as well and can in their own way be sacred.

I think of a story a woman once told me about her three-year-old daughter, Cathy, who had just started school and was having a tough time of it, and how the memories triggered by a small photograph helped that little girl to get through those early days.

"It was her teacher's idea," the woman told me. "Cathy was having difficulty separating from us and would cry herself through the day. The teacher suggested we give her a snapshot of the family to keep in her pocket so that whenever she felt lonely and far away from us she could take it out and look at it.

"A funny thing happened," she continued. "According to her teacher the first day she brought the picture to school she had a moment's pang, looked at the photo, and seemed to be okay. But throughout the rest of the day, and for the next few days, what the teacher noticed was that whenever one of those moments came upon her, Cathy would simply put her hand in her pocket, and, without bothering to take it out and look at it, feel the picture between her fingers. It seemed to do the trick. It was the feel of it that now comforted her. It was," she said, "her rosary."

Just as Cathy was comforted by her little picture and the memory it induced, any one of us might find similar comfort in similarly unexpected ways. I remember returning to the home of my youth as a young adult and happening upon a shoebox full of baseball cards, and in a moment I was back in a time when life, if it was not necessarily simpler, now seemed so. For one lifelong friend of mine it was the familiar creak of an old pew that he sat in one Christmas Eve after a long sojourn away from the church, and for another it was the aroma that stirred when, for the first time, she made a pot of soup that was a recipe she had inherited from a favorite aunt who had recently died. For another person it might be a strain of music, a work of art, an old tree house, or the tremolo of a red-throated loon one early evening at water's edge.

The point is, we are comforted in ways that remind us that there has been much good in our lives, and that there is still good to be found if only we know where and how to look for it. In a world that can at times feel so coldly indifferent, it is this comfort born of remembrance that warms our hearts.

Memory and Wisdom

Memory does more than make us warm; it also makes us wise. History, be it our own, our clan's, our nation's, or our world's, is an exacting teacher. There are a limited number of mistakes we can make in life, but when we forget history we tend to repeat them, over and over, though usually in different guises. So a parent who, as a child, picked on the weaker kids in the playground and as an adult scolds his own child unmercifully because she has brought home an A- instead of an A, has not learned from his own past that bullying is bullying, that it is counterproductive, and that it breeds resentment masquerading as respect or fear masquerading as obedience. For him memory is what the novelist Günter Grass called our "wide-mouthed sieve," so in his old age he will berate the grandchildren who do not come around often enough and beat the dog for chewing on his favorite slippers. He will live out his days alone and lonely, and blame his misery on everyone but himself.

When I think of misery writ large from lessons not learned I have to look no further than the wars my own country has engaged in just in my short lifetime. From the 54,000 American lives that were lost in Korea to the 58,000 in Vietnam, and, as of this writing, the 3,800, still mounting, who have died in Iraq, we as a nation have buried over 115,000 of our young men and women well before their time. At least one of them, Joe Matejov, was my friend, and as I write this sentence thirty-five years after his death he is still frozen in my mind as an eighteen-year-old high school kid with a mischievous smile and a lifetime of possibility in front of him. When I think of Joe's death I think too of the words of the statesman George McGovern, "I am fed up to the ears of old men dreaming up wars for young men to die in." I am left to wonder how many of these young warriors, when they were in battle, embodied the sentiment of the British poet Sigfried Sassoon, who during World War I wrote of the soldiers of his day, "when the guns begin they think of firelit homes, clean beds, and wives."

We memorialize them one and all, those who would never again return to the firelit home and the clean bed, and we have every year since the Civil War, but still we forget. We forget not only the horrors of war but the obscenity of it. We forget its waste and, more important, its futility, for as the Russian revolutionary Max Livtinov put it, today's war is only laying the groundwork for tomorrow's. Like the old man who was once the young bully, we will continue to use violence to settle differences, and continue to blame everyone but ourselves for the bloodshed.

We owe it to ourselves and, in Ezekiel's words, to our children and our children's children to learn from cruelty long past, but also to remember that it is not always delivered through the belly of a bomber or the barrel of a gun. Cruelty can just as easily present itself as an insult or a sneer, a lack of generosity or charity or respect. It is cruelty that is felt by the old woman in the small town, the one neighbors describe as "not quite right," but who is right enough to know why those neighbors cross the street whenever she is approaching, just as it is cruelty that is felt by the little boy who dreads playtime because he is always the one not chosen to play the schoolyard game.

The deeper sin here is not that we engage these behaviors as much as it is that, when we collectively choose not to remember their consequences, we perpetuate them. Prejudice looked different two hundred years ago than it does today, but it still must be spoken of in the present tense, just as the clothing that was once sewed by American children in nineteenth-century sweatshops is now sewed by Mexican kids in maquiladoros. Even the haunting whisper from Auschwitz that we must "never forget" its horrors has been either forgotten or ignored in years since in places like El Salvador, Serbia, and Darfur.

But memory *can* persist, and when it does it is often to our benefit. Like a child who stumbles upon an old toy, or an adult upon an old love letter, a prompted memory can remind us how much this thing, now forgotten, once meant to us.

David, a friend from Detroit, was visiting me in New York a little less than a year after 9/11. When I asked him whether the ripples of that event were still being felt in the Midwest, he answered candidly, "Actually, no. We are not unaware of what happened, and at the time it hit us hard. Very hard. But it seems far away now, and with each passing day it gets a little farther."

A day later David decided to head downtown to the southern tip of Manhattan, to see where the East River meets the Hudson, and to take a few pictures. Low-key tourism, he called it. That evening, when we met up for dinner and I asked him about his day he said something that surprised both of us.

"On my way down there, I of course got off at the wrong subway stop. So I decided to walk the rest of the way, feeling my way downtown," he told me. Then the words came fitfully, in staccato clips: "At one point I made a left onto a side street, and there it was. Ground Zero. It was huge. And deathly quiet. And so solemn. I had no idea. I was overcome. I shook, and I cried, and I understood why we out in Michigan don't think much about it anymore. But now I also understand why we should." David was right, of course, we should. And not only for ourselves, but for our children and our children's children.

David's trip to what he later called his wailing wall (as many of us New Yorkers called it) was a pilgrimage, inadvertent though it was, that reminds me why such journeys are important. Memory does not work if it is not stimulated, if we do not sometimes feel our way to it, turn the corner, go down that side street, and come upon something that is not part of our day-to-day experience.

When I go to the altar to receive Communion, for instance, and the bread is broken and the cup sipped "in remembrance of me," I *do* remember. In this ritual act I have turned that corner, am removed from my ordinary time and place, and transported back to an event that is bound by neither. The business of the world slips away, if only momentarily, as I again receive the meal that is my hope and my forgiveness. It need not even be this sacrament; if I am disposed to it, if I am welcoming to the notion of remembrance through ritual, then it could just as easily come to me in a communal prayer, the reading of Scripture, or a warm embrace at service's end. For that matter, if I am truly attentive, it could also come in places far away from that altar, for space is made sacred not by fiat but by how it is used, and it need not be confined to a church, a synagogue, a temple, or a mosque.

During the years of apartheid many black South Africans regularly made the trek up to a place called Table Mountain in Cape Town. It was from the top of the mountain that they could look into the sea and see Robben Island, a prison compound that once held the leadership of the African National Congress. In the days when it still served this

purpose they would go up as a show of solidarity, to let their imprisoned leaders know that they were behind them. Now, as a new South
Africa has emerged, they still go, but do so to remember the extraordinary price they had paid for justice.

In the years since then, they have brought their children to the
mountaintop, and in time, those children will bring *their* children. In
this way it will be a holy space, and the ritual of looking down to the
island, and remembering, will be their transformative moment. It will
be their sacrament, their Holy Communion, gazing upon this place
where the lambs had been fed to the wolves, where bodies were broken and blood was spilled in the name of their salvation. As Isaiah
wrote, "The wolf shall live with the lamb, the leopard shall lie down
with the kid. . . . They will not hurt or destroy on all my holy mountain; for the earth will be full of the knowledge of the LORD as the
waters cover the sea" (Isa. 11:6, 9).

But going once will not be enough, of course, which is why we go
back again and again to those rituals and to those holy places. Our
memories are fickle and fleeting, easily distracted by concerns that
are more immediate, if less important. So in this way remembering is
a discipline that we must consciously engage in, for without that discipline the memory of the important thing will lie buried among the
unpaid bills, the runny noses, and the dirty laundry. As Coleridge
said, it is "not the poem which we have read, but that to which we
return . . . possesses the genuine power."

Coleridge's words come back to me when I call to mind the dark-
est hour my own family has ever endured. When our daughter, Kate,
was fourteen years old she was seriously injured in an automobile
accident, and amid the outpouring of affection we received, a friend
sent us a small sandstone ankh, an ancient Egyptian symbol of life.
We kept it by her bedside throughout the worst of her ordeal, and
now that she is better it still hangs in her bedroom, next to her reading lamp.

I will never forget what it was like for us those first few months of
her convalescence, but, as I reacquaint myself with this much-
improved child, I do wonder if I sometimes take her recovery for
granted. With this in mind, every once in a while I go into her room
(with permission, of course; she *is* an adolescent!), pick up the ankh,

and run it through my hands. Like a little child who feels the strength of her family in the smooth gloss of a small photograph, I feel it in the abraded surface of this amulet. And it does my heart good.

Memory and Humanity

So we remember not only because we can but because we must, because God would not have it any other way. In ourselves we can see all of humanity. We are the ancient Hebrews, liberated slaves on the edge of our promised land, and we are at the table with Christ when the bread is broken and the cup is sipped. We are reluctant warriors or dedicated pacifists. We are Americans whose hearts were broken one eerily beautiful September day, and we are South Africans whose hearts were lifted when their struggle was won. We are a young girl who won her battle for life, and we are that young girl's father and mother who will never see life the same again. In memory, in remembering, we are all of these things, in all of these places.

We are also the one who keeps company with those who themselves must remember. I think back to Caroline, and I imagine her one evening, some years from now, sitting with old friends around her living room. It is the dreamy, low-lit part of the evening, when the bottle of wine is half empty, everyone has uncoiled, and they are feeling far from the worries of the world. They are telling stories, and smiling at one another with that immediate understanding, that immediate "yes, I get it" that happens between people who have known each other a long time.

Something is said and a memory is triggered. Caroline begins, "I remember a time when the two of us went out for an absolutely glorious evening. He wore his favorite suit, his blue tie, and these pearl cufflinks. . . ." Her words trail off. A tear gathers in the corner of her eye, but she is still smiling, as are they all. Because they are all there with her, in that magical moment.

As Frost also wrote in *To Earthward*, "Love at the lips was touch / As sweet as I could bear / And once that seemed too much / I lived on air."

Questions for Discussion

How has something such as a photograph, a scrapbook, or an old piece of jewelry served you as a touchstone to some distant memory?

Is it ever worthwhile to *forget*? Is it even possible?

What makes remembrance a sacred responsibility?

How can memory make us more compassionate human beings?

Chapter 5

Redemption

If you want to get the real scoop about a place you have never been to, your best bet is to talk to the people who live closest to the streets, because it is from those streets that most stories emanate and receive their wings. As Emerson wrote about his populist muse, "I embrace the common, I explore and sit at the feet of the familiar, the low. Give me insight into today, and you may have the antique and future worlds." Such was the case a number of years ago, in the small Nicaraguan city of Tipitapa, as I sat at the feet of the familiar and gained a peek into the antique and future worlds.

Back in 1989, some colleagues and I were dispatched by the United Nations to Nicaragua to serve as international observers to that country's national elections. After a dusty day spent visiting polling places, just prior to the election we headed into a local saloon. Behind the austere bar, displayed with some prominence, was an unusual icon for a place such as this, a hexagonal block of stone, machine cut, about eight inches across, and I asked the bartender about it. A sinewy little man with a thick shock of gray hair and smoky blue eyes, he was the kind of guy who looked as though he could take care of himself in a fight and rarely walked away from one.

"That stone goes back to the days of Somoza," he told me, referring to the brutal dictator Anastasio Somoza, whose politics were just to the right of Attila the Hun and whose government was kept afloat by the C.I.A. Despite hefty backing from the United States, Somoza was overthrown in 1979 by a populist revolution led by the Sandinista rebels, the success of whose rule was now to be determined by the elections we were there to observe.

"What does a stone have to do with Somoza?" I asked.

"Everything!" the man bellowed in a voice loud enough to stir the chickens languidly pecking the dirt at the back door. "And I will tell you why.

"During Somoza's reign" (he nearly spit the word "Somoza" out as he spoke, as though it was poison on his tongue, and I knew I was in for a story), "machinery was expensive but labor was cheap. *Ese cabron!* [That bastard!] Whatever the monster wanted built, he would see to it that it got built.

"And so in the late 1970s, when he wanted roads built, he had these stones manufactured and enlisted tens of thousands of slave laborers to lay them in the streets. This is how he built his roads. Instead of tar or concrete, we used these stones. They became the symbol of our oppression.

"But then the revolution started to take hold. People became bold. We took to the streets in protest, the very streets we had paved with our bare hands. And when the government tried to stop our protests by firing bullets at us," his eyes boring down on me, he spoke very slowly, as if to be absolutely certain I would hear every word, "we pulled those stones up out of the ground, and we built our barricades with them, and from behind those barricades, we fired back."

The weapons of oppression became their tools of liberation. It was a great story, and I had heard every word. But as a listener I am more obedient than incisive, so as I was about to discover, part of the lesson was lost on me.

"And so you keep the stone to remember," I said.

He smiled a broad smile that turned his eyes into taut slits and deepened even further the great furrows on his leathery face. He shook his head slowly, extended his arms to me, and turned his hands, palms up, for me to look at them. They were nothing but calluses, as rough as the stones that had made them that way. "These hands are *my* remembrances. The stone is for the generations that come after, for my kids and their friends, who don't bear the scars, who don't have the memories. It is to remind *them,* not me, why they are free, why workers get paid for their labors, and why people like you are here to observe elections that ten years ago we would have been executed for even thinking about."

I thanked him for the beer that quenched my thirst but more so for the history lesson that gave new meaning to the work that we were there to do. My friends and I then stepped out into the late afternoon sunlight.

Whether it was the beer or the story at work in my head, outside, in the heat, my thoughts left the Nicaragua of the twentieth century and traveled back thousands of years to the days of Hebrew bondage at the hands of the Egyptian pharaoh. The hard-packed streets of Tipitapa became in my mind's eye the great thoroughfares of Pithom and Rameses—also paved by slave labor—where, in the depths of their anguish, a God who had long seemed silent to a great many of them, now speaking through an intermediary they had no reason to trust, came to those slaves and promised them, "I am the LORD, and I will free you from the burdens of the Egyptians and will deliver you from slavery to them. I will *redeem* you with an outstretched arm and with mighty acts of judgment. I will take you as my people, and I will be your God" (Exod. 6:6–7).

I thought of this not only because of the affinity these brave Nicaraguans had with their Hebrew forebears, but because of the way their parallel stories of oppression and liberation are meant to be preserved. For the old man behind the bar and for his compañeros, as for those slaves to Pharaoh, the memory was etched in the coarse hands and heavy hearts they would carry with them the rest of their days. But for future generations who would not know what it was like to toil beneath the hot sun and the cracked whip for meager compensation, it was the story embedded in that small hexagonal stone, that touchstone, that cornerstone, that would provide them with a proper sense of obligation to those who had come before them.

It is no different for us, of course, because in the telling of the exodus story God instructs all of us who treat these words as our Scripture to "tell your child on that day, 'It is because of what the LORD did for *me* when *I* came out of Egypt . . . for with a strong hand the LORD brought *you* out of Egypt'" (Exod. 13:8, 9). The enslavement of our ancestors becomes our enslavement, my enslavement, as their redemption becomes ours as well. The sweat of their brow, the crust of their hands, the ache of their back, become my debt of gratitude, just as the stones they laid become my amulets, my icons of deliverance.

Ransom

To be redeemed in those ancient times meant to be bought out of slavery, a one-time economic transaction that is in Exodus given theological heft. An act of generosity granted by one human being to another defines a new sweep of history, in which the promise of God made long ago to the progenitors of these slaves is finally kept. They were a chosen people, as God had declared to their ancestral patriarchs hundreds of years earlier, but it is only now, for the first time, that God's words would receive substance in his deeds.

But if the exodus from Egypt to Canaan is to be our benchmark for divine redemption, then there is at least one conclusion we cannot escape: Freedom, even at God's hand, does not come cheap. As Jefferson put it, "We are not to expect to be translated from despotism to liberty in a featherbed." So an enraged Pharaoh met Moses' first entreaty to let his people go with the demand that they make more bricks with less straw, and from here things did not get better. The plagues followed next—frogs and flies and blood and darkness, to name but a few—culminating in the slaughter of the innocents, the death of Egyptian children whose sentence, like the sentence of slavery itself, was the consequence of an act no more criminal than the accident of birth. One tribe's savior is another tribe's executioner. No featherbeds in the tombs of the young.

But perhaps even the God of second chances became a God of second thoughts when it came to the deaths of these children, because according to the Talmud, when the next catastrophe occurred—the parting of the Red Sea and the swallowing up of Pharaoh's army— "As our rabbis taught: When the Egyptian armies were drowning in the sea, the Heavenly Hosts broke out in songs of jubilation. But God silenced them and said, 'My creatures are perishing, and you sing praises?'" (Babylonian Talmud, *Sanhedrin* 39b).

Long March to Freedom

Over the next forty years freedom took the form of hardships, miracles, promises kept and promises broken, hopes raised, dashed, and raised again. Some would lose their lives and others their faith, but as a people they soldiered on, because they were redeemed; they had rolled away the stones and were determined to procure the benefits they felt due them by virtue of the heavy price they had paid.

So they did, in Canaan, where for those who years ago had suffered under the strain of Egyptian oppression, even onerous tasks must have had a pleasing undercurrent to them. To carry a brick that was to be the foundation of *your* home must surely have made that brick feel lighter. To argue with those who govern you without fear that your demurral will be met with a whip on your back must have made monarchical governance, with all its attendant quarrels and imperfections, feel more like a lover's spat than a dance of death. Or to plant a crop for *your* consumption or to be sold at market must have made the tilling of that soil under summer's heat less oppressive. Imagine how much easier it must have been for the Nicaraguan freedom fighters to pull up those bricks than it was to lay them down. All of this is as it should be, because the first responsibility of anyone who has been granted redemption is to use it.

The Other World Wide Web

The second responsibility is to remember that none of us lives in isolation. Just as solace can be found where suffering is shared, when that suffering is lifted for one that does not mean it is lifted for all. This is why in the breaking of the Passover bread the leader of the Seder intones these hallowed words: "Among people everywhere, sharing of bread forms a bond of fellowship. For the sake of our redemption, we say together the ancient words which join us with our own people and with *all* people who are in need, with the wrongly imprisoned and the beggar in the street. For our redemption is bound up with the deliverance from bondage of people everywhere." It is also why the nineteenth-century German author Edmond Fleg wrote, "I am a Jew because in every place where suffering weeps, the Jew weeps. I am a Jew because every time despair cries out, the Jew hopes." What this means is that redemption is not a moment but a process, not just a gift but an obligation. It begins when the chains come off but does not end until all the chains, on all the slaves, in all the world, "from the imprisoned to the beggar in the street," have been cast off.

Freedom is a two-way path: we are free *from*, but we are also free *to*, and it is the world that we are released into that becomes our staging ground for the redeemed life, the world where there are still prisoners behind bars and beggars in the street. This is where our redemption must play itself out. When Martin Luther King said that "injustice anywhere is a threat to justice everywhere," he was not simply appealing to our consciences to take up a cause that is not our own. He was saying that our responsibility to those who are still victims of injustice—be it the Sudanese refugee, the Indonesian sweatshop worker, or the gay American infantryman—should be rooted in a prophetic understanding that unchecked suffering breeds unbridled contempt. There may be no more potent—and unpredictable—force on earth than an oppressed people, once organized, who are more contemptuous of their oppressors' lives than protective of their own.

We join these struggles on the side of the angels not only because it is right but because it is smart, for as King also said, "human beings are caught in an inescapable network of mutuality." When a bomb goes off in Tel Aviv its shock waves are felt in New York, and when a panhandler dies of exposure on the streets of Kiev the lives of the well-to-do in London or Paris or Madrid are also diminished, even if they never hear directly of the man's death, for they know that their wealth comes at least to some extent at the expense of others. The suffering of any person is ours as well; there is no cause that is not our own. It is not only unconscionable to refuse to seek the redemption of all people from servitude, it is shortsighted and it is foolish. As one prescient community organizer in Boston once observed to me about the underserved kids in his neighborhood, "We can build schools for now or prisons for later, it's up to us."

Promises to Keep

It was in August of 2006 that three Mexican fishermen—Jesus Vidaña, Lucio Rendon, and Salvador Ordoñez—were rescued an astonishing ten months after their small vessel was lost at sea and found five thousand miles from where their journey commenced. They were closer to Taiwan than to Mexico. It was clear from the outset that it was equal doses of ingenuity, fortitude, luck, and faith that kept them alive. One particularly touching part of the tale was a pact they made shortly before rescue, when hope was at its lowest, that if God saw fit to save their lives they would return to prayer and Scripture in order to be the kind of family men that they had heretofore failed to be. When rescue did come they were good to their word—for about a month.

Some weeks after their recovery and return to their hometown of San Blas, a reporter happened upon Rendon. "Have you been praying?" the reporter asked him. The answer was a sheepish no. Why, after making a pact with God and with God living up to his end of the bargain? "Because, honestly," Rendon answered, "I'm on land now."

Longing for rescue can turn a sinner into a saint, but the granting of it can make a liar of an honest man. When freedom comes, as it did for the Hebrews, or the Nicaraguans, or the fishermen, or any of us, it hits us the way a beam of morning light hits a long-darkened room. We are stunned by its radiance, everything looks different, and possible. Our exuberance is as boundless as our gratitude, and perhaps as irrational, and we are eager to give our lives over to God in ways that would put the most virtuous to shame. That is, until the feelings fade.

Which is what feelings do. They are like sidewalk puddles on a hot summer's day—fragile and fleeting—as are the promises we make when we are caught up in them (how many seven-year-olds promise their parents, "If you just buy me that puppy *I'll walk it every single day!*"). Only the consequences are durable. This is one of the reasons why every marriage that ends in divorce begins with vows of endless love. It is not that either spouse *intends* to breach them, but that in entering into them they must understand how difficult it is to remain faithful to a promise long after the passion of that promise has cooled and the work of marriage overrides the ease of infatuation. As Golda says of her marriage to Tevya in *Fiddler on the Roof,* "For twenty-five years I've talked with him, fought with him, starved with him. For twenty-five years my bed is his. If that's not love, what is?"

The Hebrews could not sustain their love as nobly as Golda did hers. So on Sinai they built a monument to Baal as a repudiation of the God of Moses who had redeemed them from slavery and about whom they had then sung these vows:

> The LORD is my strength and my might,
> and he has become my salvation;
> this is my God, and I will praise him,
> my father's God, and I will exalt him.
> Exod. 15:2

Their vows would have been more honest had they read, "I will exalt him until doubt overcomes faith or weakness gets the better of strength. I will exalt him until I tire of the journey and all of its privations. I will exalt him until a better offer comes along." Even with this apostasy, though, the God of second chances redeemed them again, freeing them from their self-imposed enslavement to a god of metal and pointing them anew to the promised land.

The story was similar in Nicaragua in 1989, where the Sandinistas, erstwhile darlings of the revolution, were voted out of office because, despite having defeated Somoza, they could not defeat double-digit unemployment, polluted drinking water, or a lack of school supplies. The citizens figured they got a better offer.

Redemption's value is proportionate to its sturdiness, which is less a function of the magnitude of the gesture than of the seriousness with which we receive it. The recovering drug addicts and alcoholics I have worked with have taught me plenty about addiction. The one point they make without fail is that even though sobriety may begin with a fresh rush of determination, the real work comes in the day-to-day, the tedious, tiresome, endless labor of *remaining* dry. This is why they say they are *in* recovery, not recovered, because there is no point at which they have defeated the addiction. A poignant illustration of this came from a patient who had been at an AA meeting the night before:

"There was a lot of talk from two young guys about how well they were doing because it had been about six months since their last drink, and neither had ever stayed sober that long," he told me. "Then, in the back of the room, an elderly woman stood up, and looked at them both, and said, 'Young men, I'm eighty-six years old. I had my last sip of alcohol sixty-three years ago. Until last night, that is, when I single-handedly finished off a fifth of vodka. I'm still eighty-six, and I've been sober one day. You see, I'm an alcoholic.'"

This woman's extraordinary story is her testimony to the fact that if she is to remain redeemed, freed from the hold the poison once had over them, she must accept the fact that there is no Canaan; her wilderness wandering will be lifelong. She was telling the young men that their ability to endure, to live with their disease rather than die from it, would be largely determined by their willingness to accept that they will never be "cured" of alcoholism, never reach a promised land. While their experiences of addiction may be foreign to many of us, their approach to redemption is instructive to all of us. As Bill Wilson, the founder of AA, put it, the story of the recovering addict "is the story of suffering transmuted, under grace, into spiritual progress."

Blessed Are Those Who Have Not Seen

If there is one person in all of Christian history I envy it is Doubting Thomas. Invited by the risen Christ to put his fist in Christ's wounded side and run his fingers over Christ's pierced hands, nobody was given more assurance that the resurrection really happened, that life was victorious over death, that humanity had been redeemed, than Thomas.

The days that followed the death and resurrection of Jesus were not easy for the ragged remnant that would eventually become the Christian church. They had more enemies than friends, their lives were in constant danger. It had been a hard three years, and there was no reason to believe the coming years would be any easier. Surely there were times they wanted to throw up their hands in exhaustion and admit that building a community of believers around the memory of a man who had vowed to turn the social and religious order on its head, and had died trying, had about as much chance of bearing fruit as a mustard seed in the Sinai desert. But if anyone had the wherewithal to weather them it was Thomas.

I picture Thomas sitting there quietly, in the midst of these frustrations, extending his fingers or balling them into a fist, remembering what it felt like, to touch those wounds in which he found his resolve. Like the Nicaraguan barkeep feeling his own callous-creased hands, it is easier to remember the promise of freedom when you cannot forget its cost.

The harder part comes to those of us who follow, who are inheritors of the redeeming act but who were not there when it was first enacted. Faith is always harder than certainty, and belief in the power of a distant God is easily shaken by discouraging events that are as close as our own front door.

We read of manna falling from heaven but look around on earth and see that one-third of the population is malnourished or starving. The prophet sings praises to a God he calls the "Everlasting Father, Prince of Peace" (Isa. 9:6), but we cannot help but wonder if a lasting peace will ever come and cure us of our proclivity to treat war as though it is a first choice rather than a last resort. When Jesus assures me that "you will weep and mourn . . . you will have pain, but your pain will turn into joy" (John 16:20), my thoughts turn to people I know who have by all accounts done everything right in their lives but are still visited by pain so profound that I am not sure what gets them on their feet in the morning, let alone on their knees at night.

I never put my fist in the wounded side of Christ or laid a stone in a street at the order of a tyrant or lifted it up in defiance of the same. But I am the inheritor of the story of redemption, of freedom, and though I know that there will be times when I forget that story, I know too that my God will not forget me. Like the first spring crocuses timidly peeking out from under their blanket of winter's frost, I will glimpse the signs. An old person who has lived a full life will tell me that he has no fear of death, that he welcomes it, and I will hear in his voice the freedom that will be his company for this one last journey. A woman will extricate herself from an abusive relationship, and I will believe without reservation that she possesses the strength to never subject herself to that horror again. Total strangers will drop what they are doing and gather themselves in a mud-caked lot, and a house will rise defiant in Biloxi, Mississippi, or Laboi, Indonesia. And just as I felt the clouds of despair gathering to surround me, they break, and a blue sky blankets a cool earth, and again I feel redeemed.

The Good in the Bad

One more quality of biblical redemption bears mention here, and that is the redemption of the self by the self. No one's life is a perfect arc reaching ever-heavenward. Bad things happen to us for no reason, with no warning, and for which we are therefore generally ill prepared (God does not tell everyone when it is time to build an ark). When they do happen they carry with them their own metaphoric enslavement characterized by a sense of sadness or anger or fear or confusion or despair or all of the above. Unlike the enthusiasm of the newly liberated, these feelings cling to us leech-like, consume us, and rob us of both energy and hope. The bad thing might come in the form of a lost job or a lost love. Or perhaps it is a shadow on an X-ray, graffiti on our house of worship, or an unanswered outreach to an estranged friend who by her silence is telling us that she intends to stay that way.

The question we are tempted to ask is why this happened to us, but the more useful question is what we can do with it. The eighty-six-year-old alcoholic who gave testimony in the AA meeting redeemed her failure to stay sober by using it as a cautionary tale to the two young men who were too quick to congratulate themselves for their own brief sobriety. She put that failure to use in the service of another, and we can all do the same.

My friends, a middle-aged couple named Walter and Patty, are two of the kindest persons to ever walk the face of the earth. They were crushed when their young son Michael died of a heart attack just short of his twenty-sixth birthday. A year after his death, Walter talked about how the past year had changed the family:

"There's one thing both Patty and I notice now. It's subtle, but unmistakable. Whenever we talk on the phone, either to each other, to our own siblings, or to our [surviving] kids, we always end the conversation by saying 'I love you' to one another. Other families may have always done that, but we never did, and it's not as though we made a pact with one another to do it now. We've just slipped into the habit. Patty thinks it's really our way of saying 'I'll never take you for granted,' and I think she's right. And if she is, it's really our way of telling ourselves that Michael will always remind us just how fortunate we are to have one another in our lives, and that we are wise never to forget that."

The Zen of Redemption

The paradox of redemption is that it comes to us in our weakness but is dependent upon our strength. We are bought out of slavery by another, but when the cuffs come off it is our responsibility to keep them off. The road is hard and temptations great, but we do not engage the struggle ill equipped. If nothing else we carry into battle the memory—be it ours or that of others who came before us—of the weight of those cuffs and the toll that they take on body and soul. If we cannot run our fingers over our own calluses, or cannot put those fingers into our own Savior's wounds, we can at least know the story that bears testimony to both the origin and the worth of those wounds. We can know too, in appreciation, that they are the price paid for our freedom.

Questions for Discussion

Does redemption make suffering worthwhile? Does it make suffering useful?

Are there experiences in your life that roughly parallel, if only symbolically, the enslavement of the Hebrews at the hands of Pharaoh?

Why is it hard to sustain the gratitude we feel when we have been redeemed, and what can we do about this?

Chapter 6

Revelation

When living true to the wonder of the steadily unfolding wisdom we feel at time as if the echo of an echo of a voice were piercing the silence, trying in vain to get our attention.
—Abraham Joshua Heschel

*I*t is a deep, crisp August night high in the southern Adirondack Mountains, and my friend Henry and I are lying on the beach outside his cottage watching aurora borealis. The northern lights dance silently and playfully across the moonless summer sky. Their rhythmic, oscillating motions and brilliant colors of blue and red and green hold us in silent sway for several minutes, finally broken only by Henry's long, reverent, if semiliterate, "Coooooool!" A few more words are exchanged, and then at one point Henry has what "seems like a good idea at the time."

"The guy in the cabin next to mine, Lloyd, is a retired astrophysicist from Columbia University. I'll bet if we get him out here he can tell us what's really going on up there!"

It *did* seem like a good idea, but then he let it steep for another moment, and said, "Actually, let's not do that. Right now this is a pretty jaw-dropping experience. I get Lloyd out here and I know what's gonna happen. It's gonna become a science class; ions, atmospheric pressure, electromagnetic fields, and all that other stuff. Maybe we're better off just enjoying the visuals and leaving it at that."

I muttered something about how kids would rather *not* know how the magician made the lady in the box disappear, and how this was pretty much of a kid moment for us, and we left well enough alone. It was sufficient to be dazzled that night; we could wait for another time to be educated.

Had Henry and I been born centuries earlier, long before scientists like Lloyd were around to demystify nature as only scientists can, we might have considered that evening's entertainment something of a divine revelation, as though with one great sweep of his hand God deigned to impress two lowly New Yorkers with his majesty, his might, and his flair for primary colors. But we were not. We are products of the scientific age. So, as glorious as it was to behold, it was decipherable.

But this is how revelation works, how the divine is made known to us. Revelation is the indecipherable being put into words. In Scripture it is God revealing his intent, his teaching, his Tao, to the prophet. The prophet in turn is the one who is metaphorically lying beneath that summer night's sky, drinking in that intent, and whose burden it is to find words to communicate to his people the essence behind what has been communicated to him.

It is written in Exodus that "God *called* to [Moses] . . ." (3:4), just as in Jeremiah we read, "Thus *said* the LORD to me . . ." (13:1), and in Amos, "the LORD roars from Zion, and *utters* his voice from Jerusalem . . ." (1:2). But when the prophet writes such things we do ourselves no favor to take it literally, as if God's Word came in the form of word, sound, speech, rather than as a transcendent event that defies replication. As the great medieval philosopher and physician Moses Maimonides wrote of revelation in his masterpiece, *The Guide of the Perplexed*, "The perception by the senses . . . is best known to us; we have no idea or notion of any other mode of communication between the soul of one man and that of another man except by means of speaking." He adds, however, "our minds are merely to receive a notion that there is a divine knowledge to which the prophets attain. . . . We must not suppose that in speaking God employed voice or sound." He then goes on to add that the perception of God's will by the prophet is not a perception of the eye or ear, but a "spiritual perception."

The importance here is not to diminish revelation but to revere it by honoring the depth of its mystery. As Abraham Heschel observed, the words "And God said, let there be light" evoke an inner response to an ineffable meaning. "It was not essential that [God's] will be transmitted as sound; it *was* essential that it be made known to us. The sound or sight is to the transcendent event what a metaphor is to an abstract principle." Revelation does not unmask God's mystery so much as it contains and therefore underscores it.

But Why Be Made Known to Us?

Our God is a God of history, not of theory or abstraction. God's purpose in revelation is not to teach us of his essence but of his actions, to remind us that he is the Creator who seeks us out (Gen. 3:9: "The LORD called to Adam, and said to him, 'Where are you?'") and weaves himself into our lives in very real, concrete, and personal ways. His concern is not of heavenly things but of earthly ones, which is why the Bible begins as it does, with the creation of the earth and all that is in it. It is also why, in a syntactical subtlety lost in English, when he is giving the Hebrews the Ten Commandments, and they begin with "I am the Lord your God," the word "your" is singular, not plural. It is the prophet's way of telling us of God's immediacy to us, that he directs himself not to the world as a collective thing but to each one of us individually. He is the Lord *my* God, the Lord *your* God. It is revelation of another kind, as it makes known to us the depth of God's intimacy with us.

We will never fully know God because the infinite is forever beyond the reach of the finite, but we will always have full access to God's presence on earth if we open ourselves to the world around us and our place in it. It is, as Blake wrote, "To see a World in a Grain of Sand and a Heaven in a Wild Flower. Hold Infinity in the palm of your hand, an Eternity in an hour." This is how God speaks to us, be it through a grain of sand or a starry night.

Quid Pro Quo

Just as the stars do not reveal unless they are seen, the word of God does not speak to us unless it is heard. Revelation is not revelation without human perception and human response, because something can be defined as having been given only if it is then taken. Thus it is that to God's revelation to Moses at Sinai the people say "everything that the LORD has spoken, we will do" (Exod. 19:7). Or, as Heschel put it, "In our response to His will we perceive His presence in our deeds. His will is revealed in our doing. In carrying out a sacred deed we unseal the wells of faith." This is both a definition and a challenge of faith; it helps us understand revelation, but part of that understanding is the admission that as we discover the word of God it is our imperative to answer it, and it is an imperative we do not always rise to. This is why the very word *revelation* is used, because it derives from the Latin *re velare*, which means "to pull back the veil." The implication is that though it might be offered often we are not always quick to see or to receive the word from God.

We come by this hesitance honestly; it is not the sole purview of those of us of feeble faith. Remember, Sarah, Abraham's wife and "at an advanced age," laughed incredulously when God told her she would soon bear a child, and Moses demurred when God ordered him to lead his people out of Egypt, asking that his brother Aaron stand in his stead. Jesus at Gethsemane prayed that if there were any way that the burden of salvation could be lifted from his shoulders he would welcome it. That same night, when the love of a friend could have supplied some comfort for the pain he endured, the apostle Peter denied even knowing the man he had not long before called his Lord and Christ.

Such reluctance is as often as not simply a product of the sheer immensity of the experience, of God's making himself known to us. Divine revelation, whether heard as unfolding promise or impending threat, is nothing if not momentous. Before God promised Noah a rainbow he threatened him a flood, neither of which Noah could regard with anything less than knee-buckling awe. God's intentions, while perhaps inscrutable, are nevertheless very real, and we must bear their consequences for good or ill on our reluctant shoulders, no small order. So whether he is telling the disobedient Syrians through the prophet Amos that "for three transgressions of Damascus, and for four, I will not revoke the punishment; because they have threshed Gilead with threshing sledges of iron" (1:3), or the frightened shepherds in

Luke that "to you this day is born in the city of David a Savior" (2:11), or the whole world, through John, that a time is coming when "he will wipe away every tear from their eyes. Death will be no more" (Rev. 21:4), we must hear the words as if directed to us and overcome whatever hesitancies we might harbor because only that way do we close the circle and make the revelation a completed thing.

On the other hand, perhaps it is not the immensity of the experience but quite the opposite that gives us pause. When Amos prophesied against Syria and "the transgressions of Damascus," his words were received with a solemnity befitting their source. But that oracle was given nearly three thousand years ago, in a very different part of the world, in a language that outside of scholarly circles is no longer spoken, to a man we know little about, in a manner shrouded in mystery that has not even been remotely replicated in our lifetimes. How are we to receive it with the same reverence as the prophet who experienced it, or the people to whom it was addressed and for whose lives it had immediate bearing?

The answer of course is that we probably cannot. But that does not preclude us from hearing it as the revealed word within which there is a contained truth, just as within us is contained the power of a faithful response. We do not live in ancient Damascus, but we do not have to reach any farther than the prisons at Guantánamo Bay or the gulags of apartheid South Africa to appreciate Amos's words of warning against a conquering nation that treats its adversaries inhumanely— in this instance the people of Gilead—by beating them "with sledges of iron."

If we regard Scripture as revelation, then it is our responsibility to open ourselves to it such that the words first transmitted thousands of years ago do not diminish over time and distance but travel that great sweep of history to find their way into our consciousness, our soul, and our daily lives. In Judaism the moment that God revealed himself at Sinai is referred to in two classical terms, *mattan torah* and *kabbalat torah*, the first being "the giving of torah" and the second "the acceptance of torah," and this is precisely the moment we are faced with in our own confession of faith: Do we accept the scripturally revealed word and make manifest that acceptance in our hearts, minds, words, and deeds, or do we not?

If we do, we find meaning in the barbarity of the Damascans so many eons ago because their story speaks to the ease with which victors can come to see their victims as something less than human and in so doing exhibit a timeless condescension not befitting a person of faith or a principled society. In this way people of any era—ourselves included—can find life in these dust-encrusted words from the mouth of an ancient prophet long dead who received them in a vision from a God he never saw. They are not just commentary on an empire that no longer exists or even on contemporary empires that make the mistake of disrespecting cultures they deem lesser than themselves. They also remind us of our obligation not to disrespect people who we deem lesser than ourselves, people who have not had our good fortune, or people who have, or who have even at some time in their lives enjoyed greater fortunes than we will ever know but who, for whatever reasons, squandered their opportunities and are now the worse off for it.

My childhood friend Robert, a successful New York architect, was born into a working-class family, worked in the family deli as a kid, and was the first of his generation to attend college. A few weeks prior to a recent get-together we had scheduled, he saw a former classmate of ours, a star high school athlete named Gary who had been inordinately popular and insufferably arrogant.

"I was in a restaurant having dinner with some clients," Bob began, "and who should I see bussing the tables but Gary. He used to knock my books out of my hands when I was hurrying to class, or cuff me in the back just to humiliate me. Now here he was, cleaning up after me. I didn't introduce myself, though I thought about it. I figured if he was the same guy today that he was thirty-five years ago, he'd be smart enough to see the irony but also to be embarrassed. He didn't need that." I admired my old friend's decision and thought I might have been more Damascan than Samaritan in my handling of the situation.

The words that speak of God's revelation and our response are there, should we choose to pull back the veil and see them, even if the message is embedded in long-ago events and faraway places. It is not only a call to justice for conquered people that emanates from these ancient pages; the generosity of divine revelation is commensurate with the multiplicity of human need. So it is that when I read in the

Psalms, "The earth is the LORD's and all that is in it" (24:1), I am both heartened by the limitlessness of God's dominion and compelled to be a proper steward of it. When the author of Ecclesiastes tells me that "better is a poor and wise youth than an old but foolish king" (4:13), my faith in the innocent and suspicion of the powerful are revived. When I read in the Gospel of John, "Do not let your hearts be troubled, and do not let them be afraid" (14:27), and know they are coming from a man who had every reason to carry the weight of a troubled, frightened heart, I am touched to my core by his assurances that my world will hold together even as his is tearing apart. When Paul entreats me to live a life of "compassion, kindness, humility, meekness, and patience. Bear with one another and, if anyone has a complaint against another, forgive each other" (Col. 3:12), I realize that in some instances the veil is so thin as to be easily penetrated.

In Everyday Places

I do not believe we diminish the authority of the revealed word by contemplating the notion of God's making himself known to us through mediums that lie beyond the confines of our sacred books. As the iconoclastic theologian Paul Tillich once observed, God came to us in the form of a human being but can "just as easily have come in the form of a stick or a stone." I believe God's openness to us can be more easily presumed than our openness to God.

There is a wonderful old rabbinic tale of openness that centers around a once-thriving monastery somewhere in Eastern Europe that has fallen on hard times. In desperation, the monastery's abbot pays a visit to seek the advice of a wise rabbi he knows.

The abbot told the rabbi his story of how, at one time, his monastery had been famous throughout the Western world, but now was all but desolate and, to add insult to injury, falling apart. Visitors did not come, only a handful of monks remained, and they were not happy.

"Is it because of some sin of ours that the monastery has been reduced to this state?" the abbot asked, to which the rabbi answered, "Yes, the sin of ignorance. You see, one among you is the Messiah in disguise, and you're ignorant of this." That was all he said on the matter.

On the trek back to the monastery, the abbot wracked his brain over who in their midst could be the Messiah. Brother Frank? No, gentle, but dim. Brother Thomas? No, too quick to anger. Brother Joseph? No, too easily despairing. On the other hand, he thought, the rabbi *did* say the Messiah would be in disguise, so perhaps his defects were his disguise! Come to think of it, everyone in the monastery had defects, and one of them had to be the Messiah!

Back in the monastery he assembled the monks and told them what he had learned, and they looked at one another in disbelief. The Messiah? Here? Hard to believe. But he was supposed to be there in disguise. Because they wanted to do right by the Messiah but did not know who it was, they decided to play it safe, so they took to treating everyone with tremendous respect and consideration. "You never know," they said to themselves when they dealt with one another, "maybe this guy is the one."

The result of this was that over time the atmosphere in the monastery became vibrant with joy. In time dozens of aspirants were seeking admission to the order. People returned to bask in their loving glow. They rebuilt their little chapel with mortar and timber—the stick and the stone—and their community was reborn. They had their second chance.

The point of this little fable is, of course, that when we open ourselves to the possibility of God being revealed we will not only perceive the revelation, we will participate in it. It was in the end the monks who rolled back the veil, and what did they find but their Messiah, their salvation, in their very midst.

We are those pre-salvation monks insofar as we fail to hear what Elijah heard as "a sound of sheer silence" (1 Kgs. 19:12), so drowned out it is by the static buzz of trifling necessities and petty disappointments that crowd so much of our lives. We go through a particularly bad week when we are outraged by a newspaper headline, anxious about a medical checkup, frustrated over a report card, and irritated by what a neighbor's dog has done to our lawn. Come Sunday we sit in our house of worship hoping for respite, but at least on this particular Sabbath the preacher is pedantic, the choir is flat, and the prayers are skewed toward gratitude when what we were hoping for was a dose of righteous anger with a side order of lament. We get outside, there is a dent in our fender, and it has started to rain. The veil feels more like a wet blanket; God is nowhere to be heard from.

It is moments like these that we do well to remember that the only permanent fact of life is that nothing in life is permanent. A story goes that a great knight was captured by an enemy king, who threatened to put the warrior to death at daybreak but promised to set him free if he could provide the king, in his words, "with something that makes me happy when I am sad and sad when I am happy." At dawn the next day the knight handed the king a piece of paper. The king read it, and ordered him released. On the paper the knight had simply written, "This too shall pass."

I do not know that we have to treat life's incivilities with stoic calm and steely reserve, but I do not believe we have to treat them as evidence of God's absence. Even when Jesus prayed in vain that the cup be taken from him, his petitions were Godward, as was Jeremiah's lament that "my eyes flow with tears, for a comforter is far from me," and David's dissent in Psalm 42, "Why have you forgotten me? Why must I walk about mournfully because the enemy oppresses me?" Sometimes the most heartfelt prayer is the one we pray with the least faith that it will be answered, which is why it can be so gratifying when it is. As often as not that answer contains as much revelation as it does mystery, offering less of what we want than what we need, from a God who reminds us that our sufferings are no more a function of his absence than our riches are of his presence, a God, in Paul's words, viewed only "through a glass darkly."

Be Careful What You Ask For

Finally, I believe there are times when revelation impinges on us in ways more disquieting than assuring, when the veil is pulled back but we do not like what we see. It was the irrepressible Protestant minister Harry Emerson Fosdick who once observed in a children's sermon, "If God is so good, why does he put the vitamins in spinach instead of ice cream?" Put another way, why is it that when we ask our faith to be a source of satisfaction it instead comes back to us a mandate to feed the poor, clothe the naked, end war, save the planet, endure our unsatisfied desires and insufficient paychecks, or show kindness to some sidewalk stranger who will never thank us for it? The short answer is that there is gratification to be found in noble acts, but the long answer is that we need to distinguish between ephemeral pleasures and enduring joys. By which I mean faith does not inure us from life's pains or entitle us to its thrills, but it does assure us that whatever life's content at any given moment, be we feather-floating on the winds of fortune or lead heavy with the weight of the world, there is a God beyond description who loves us beyond words, and whose love, unlike all else in life, shall not pass.

To What Is True

Our journey through life has much to do with separating the real from the counterfeit and coming to understand—however dimly—the substance and meaning of the divine made known to us. We want to be illuminated, though not by false lights or fleeting stars that burn hot white with promise but only for a moment before leaving us again in the dark. We must ask God to incline our hearts to what is true.

Many years ago the town of Rochester, New York, was illuminated by just such a false light. One symbol of God's revealing truth in the town was the cross that sat atop the steeple of the Irondiquoit Congregational Church, and during World War II the church received an odd gift from a local manufacturer of lenses. The war had been good to the manufacturer and he was flush with money, so to beautify the church at night he offered to illuminate the great cross. It was only years later that congregants discovered the truth. The manufacturer had done this not to cast light where there was once darkness, and not to glorify God. He did it so the cross could be seen from the roof of his plant, where late-shift workers would use it as a target to test the accuracy of the night sites they were assembling for military rifles. He had turned the ultimate symbol of God's revealing love into an instrument that did not so much conquer death as place its power in human hands. This is a useful reminder that as we endeavor to lift the veil in search of a God whose peace passes all understanding, we ourselves understand the need to recognize the difference between true peace and false promises, between a God being made known and the devil in disguise.

True peace is God revealed in ways that render him simultaneously imminent and transcendent, the mystery at one and the same moment both unveiled and preserved. It is two friends on a warm summer's night sitting under the stars on a beach not far from Rochester, New York, and gazing stupidly into the sky, watching majestic splashes of color that they know have a scientific explanation but surrender instead to the wordless wonder. Elijah could do no better than "the voice of silence." These two do no better than "Cooooool!" But it will suffice.

Questions for Discussion

Has our understanding of science made it less likely for us to find God revealed in our natural surroundings?

Is God still revealed to us today the way he was during biblical times?

Can God be revealed to us through Scriptures? Through texts that are not scriptural?

Is there a danger in people misunderstanding or misinterpreting events as moments of divine revelation when they are something else altogether?

Chapter 7

Resurrection

Religion is a wizard, a sibyl. She faces the wreck of worlds and prophesies restoration. She faces a sky blood red with sunset colors that deepen into darkness and prophesies dawn. She faces death and prophesies life.

—Felix Adler

*T*here is a wonderful old Celtic legend that is about as believable as a barroom boast but is dead-eyed honest when it comes to depicting the indomitability of the Irish spirit. As the story goes, back in the days when Ireland chafed under British rule even more so than they do today, insurgents would go from town to town to stir up the spirit of rebellion among the locals.

The roads these insurrectionists traveled were hazardous, so they would often travel them at night when it was more difficult for their enemy to spot them. To sustain themselves, they would tie little pouches of corn kernels to their belts so they could eat and walk at the same time.

They were often successful, but just as often they were not, and it was not uncommon to hear of one brave man or another captured by British soldiers or loyalists on, say, the road from Galway to Kilkenny or Killarney to Cork. Instead of taking the man prisoner, the soldiers would kill him and bury his body in a shallow grave by the side of the road, and his death would be made to serve as a lesson that resistance to the crown was futile, because British rule was in Ireland to stay.

But the one thing the British did not figure on were those little pouches of corn, because the following spring, wherever a brave Irishman had lost his life for the good of the cause, those kernels would take root and sprout. Great green shoots would coax their way out of the rich country loam, timid at first, but then growing boldly heavenward, to sway in the wind like the palms of the pilgrims upon Jesus' entry into Jerusalem. These stalks bear witness to a divine promise that though their oppressors could kill the flesh, they could not kill the spirit, and there are those romantics who believe to this day that this was why, in 1798, the British finally outlawed the color green.

You can outlaw a color but you cannot outlaw an idea. You can kill a man who stands for a noble principle but you cannot kill a living principle, because death does not defeat life. If anything, as in the case of this folktale, death can both ennoble and embolden life. At its heart this is the promise of the resurrection story, of Christ overcoming death; it is to declare that darkness does not have the final say. It is a declaration made not only in grand gestures where life literally hangs in the balance as it did on the cross that fateful Friday, but in the small and sometimes unremarkable places where so much of life is lived unnoticed.

Lives and Deaths

To overcome death, even death writ small, means first to acknowledge its existence as a brooding, hovering presence more sensed than seen or heard, like an unwelcome guest who invites himself into our home but promises to busy himself in a far-off corner and speak little or not at all so as not to interrupt the party. It is in this way that we experience not Death per se but deaths, endings, final chapters that can bring with them a sense of satisfied completion, but can just as easily (if paradoxically) burden us with a sense of sadness, however profound or faint.

So it is when, for instance, a good neighbor of many years finds work in a faraway town. Although your relationship need not die with his move, the relationship *as you have known it* must. No more impromptu two-family back porch summer meals, no more late-night bull sessions about the impenetrable mysteries of pyramids, parenthood, or the perfect golf swing, no one to gather your mail and watch your home when you travel, or run to the pharmacy when someone is ill. When they are set to leave you, you are stoic; both of you hide your sorrows behind thin veneers of corny humor and well-intentioned assurances that you will "keep in touch." But deep inside what you feel more intensely than anything is the unhappiness that accompanies certain loss and the hard-edged knowledge that things will be forever different.

If it is not a friend who has left the neighborhood, it is a child, now grown, who has left the home. Or perhaps it is the old spruce tree in the backyard, the one that child in her youth so loved to climb, that has finally lost its battle with age and illness. Or maybe it is none of these deaths that happen outside ourselves, maybe it is a passage more intrinsic to us. We are cleaning out the attic one day and we discover that our wedding suit has somehow miraculously shrunk from what it was when first we wore it those many years ago when we were so handsome and full of hope. We also notice that our gait has slowed on our morning run, and we are shaving a little distance off as well. The hairs on our head are grayer, and thinner. We look out the window at the stump that was once that old spruce and we begin to wonder how close or distant we are from its fate. It is not a consuming thought, but it does come around from time to time, drifting away then circling back, and for now it is enough to swat it away like a gnat at a picnic, for we are determined not to let it spoil our good time.

It is these and countless other little deaths, these lower-case passages through time and experience, that serve to remind us that nothing is permanent and that our contentment in life—while dependent upon many things—is directly proportionate to the grace with which we accept that impermanence. I think of the Buddhist priests who labor for weeks or months over a mandala, the intricate and breathtakingly beautiful sand art that they create one grain at a time, and then, upon completion, pour it into the river so as to symbolize the impermanence of everything, the inevitability of passage, and the danger of attachment. The question we must ask ourselves is not how to avoid these passages—which is like asking the earth at noonday to avoid that evening's sunset—but how to use them. As one Zen master put it to me: How do we die creatively?

Creative Death

I think one of the subtexts of the master's question has to do with what we can learn from our passages, and I think one of the answers is that we learn to find value in that which is now a part of our history. We learn to listen to the ghosts, glean their wisdom, and take something of the old with us into the new. The loss could be good or bad, could be imposed or chosen, could be a product of the inevitable or the accident of coincidence. From our first tooth, to our innocence, to our livelihood, whatever the substance, every loss offers some lesson if we only know how to forage for it.

For my old boyhood friend Peter, summer was not summer without the Saturday morning baseball game. Peter's is a life lived with no more or less than his share of satisfactions and disappointments, steady and stable if unremarkable. But in his adulthood he looked forward to those games the way a kid looks forward to summer camp—eagerly, and single-mindedly, knowing that however formidable that week's problems might be, for these few sacred hours joy will come with the toss of the ball, the crack of the bat, and the dignity of a dirty uniform. Peter put it well when, in trying to explain to his young daughter the pleasure he got from this weekly ritual, he simply said, "Honey, life is complicated. Baseball isn't."

This was something that he truly loved, so much so that I cannot even begin to wonder how he felt when, on his fiftieth birthday no less, the orthopedist told him that the injury he had sustained in a skiing accident meant giving baseball up for good.

A few years after he received the deflating news, and with summer fast approaching, I gingerly asked Peter how he was getting along without the game. Never one to be dismissive, he considered his answer long and hard before he spoke, and then he said, "I would be lying to tell you anything less than that I miss it terribly. But I have to admit, begrudgingly, some good has come out of it, if at a price I'd rather not have been made to pay." I told him I thought he was entitled to his grudges, and he did not disagree.

"I still go and watch the guys play," he then said. "I didn't think I'd want to; I thought it would be too painful to sit there like the kind of stone we'd dig out of the infield dirt and toss onto the sidelines. The impediment. I didn't care to be something extraneous and in the way. But I've come to realize that a big part of the enjoyment of the game has to do with something other than playing. To be out under that rich blue sky, the morning sun, the smell of the grass, and most of all to be surrounded by my buddies, all in all it's not a bad compromise." Then, with a glint and a smile, he added, "Life still is complicated, and baseball still isn't."

This was Peter's resurrection moment, his creative death, because he took something of the old into the new. He did not try to bury his grief, but he did not let it bury him either. Had he not played this game with these men for those many years I do not believe he would have enjoyed sitting and watching them play it now. But having done so he could still cheer a good swing of the bat, still ridicule a booted ground ball, still swap postgame lies that, like Irish legends, tell about the youthful glory years that never were.

Dying into Life

But beyond the wisdom we gain from where we have been, there is something even more about creative death than this, and it has to do not only with what we preserve of the past but where we take it. It has to do with exiting one room so as to enter another. It has to do with dying *into* something.

I am always thunderstruck by the fortitude I see exhibited by brave women who have found their way out of abusive relationships, largely because in their liberation they recognize that not only have they changed their circumstances, they have changed themselves. Their circumstances have changed because they no longer suffer the degradation of their abuser. They have changed because they now understand that they are no longer burdened by those pieces of their own character that unwittingly capitulated to the abuse. They have died to the moniker of victim and been resurrected to that of survivor. They have prevailed. What this means is that they have gone through not one passage but several, because not only have they dissolved a poisonous relationship, they have also come face-to-face with those parts of themselves that made them susceptible to such a relationship in the first place. With the tremendous pain that is inherent in any such unvarnished self-examination, they have freed themselves from their demons, both within and without.

Theirs is a form of death insofar as they have given up something of themselves, however unhealthy. But it is a creative death because they have taken the lessons of their experience and forged from that experience a stronger, wiser, and more vibrant woman. Having been beaten down for so long, having died to that inherent sense of self-worth with which we are all naturally imbued at birth, they have res-urrected themselves (literally *re-surrectionem*, or "risen again") by reclaiming that worth. Eyes forever downcast now look skyward with a sense of stiff-spined confidence and well-placed optimism. With ee cummings in his immortal poem "i thank You God for most this amazing day," they can sing unabashedly that they who have died are alive again in "the gay, great happening illimitably earth." Their earth is again illimitable.

I think of Jesus' appearances after his resurrection ("I who have died and am alive again") as nothing if not affirmations of that illimitability, because to a world overcome with unspeakable dark-ness he brought unbearable light. By the account of the Gospel according to John, to Thomas's doubts he brought assurance ("Put your finger here and see my hands. . . . Do not doubt but believe," 20:27), to the disciples' fears he brought peace ("Peace be with you. As the Father has sent me, so I send you," 20:21), and to Mary's crippling sadness he brought compassion ("Woman, why are you weeping? Whom are you looking for?" 20:15). Assurance, peace, and compassion: faith, hope, and love—these are the very keystones of life as a glint in the eye of God, the very font whence life can arise from death.

Put another way, to his people, whose discouragement was bot-tomless, he gave a world of second chances. This small band of erst-while, reluctant believers, who in Thoreau's words would have otherwise lived out their lives in quiet desperation, instead went forth defiant of impossible odds to lay the foundation of a church that—despite the maddening flaws and endless shortcomings it has shown over the years and continues to show to this day—still proclaims his name and divines his work. That work is nothing if not the work of rising again, of creating: out of doubt, faith; out of despair, hope; and out of hatred, love.

Creatio ex Nihilo

It is, I believe, the artist who most eloquently expresses that creative human power, who, at his or her best, harnesses but does not tame it, and then presents it to us such that the creativity is not just seen but beheld, felt, absorbed, finally spiraling down to a wordless place, a place where we are left only to gasp in awe, deep within our very bones. The seventeenth-century French genius François Girardon was a brilliant sculptor whose work was commissioned by Louis XV to adorn the grounds of Versailles. Girardon had a gift for taking an inert slab of dolomite marble and creating bold pieces that played upon the entire gamut of human emotion, often ironically but never contradictorily or without intention.

So to walk the grounds of the great palace is to have your senses delighted by the floating ethereal lightness of his playful *Bathing Nymphs*, then suddenly jolted into anger by his *Rape of Prosperine*, and just as abruptly moved to tears by the pathos you see etched in the weeping face of an old man in *Winter*. In each piece Girardon is opening up our emotions to the great risks and rewards inherent in being human. By doing this as a sculptor—by taking lifeless blocks of stone, dead rock, breathing such depth of life into them, and by extension deepening the lives of those who will behold them—he becomes, wittingly or otherwise, a symbol for us of the power of resurrection even in the hands of a mere mortal.

We are, of course, all artists in our own right, all endowed with the power to breathe life into stone. But to do so means taking risks of our own. After all, what was it if not risk buttressed by faith that fortified a bunch of ordinary people marching for racial equality in 1965 to rise up after being knocked to the ground by Alabama jackboots on the Edmund Pettus Bridge and to continue their trek to Montgomery? What was it if not risk that spurred the gays at New York's Stonewall bar to finally resist police harassment in 1969 and birthed the gay rights movement? What do these and other acts of courage yield if not new life for the beaten down? Resurrection as art—the art of disobeying the powers that be when it is the wont of those powers to stifle creativity in the interest of preserving conformity.

Some years ago in the poorest neighborhood of New York City, a section of northern Harlem (known locally as Bradhurst) that suffered from double-digit unemployment and a per capita income under $6,500, a homegrown clergyman by the name of Preston Washington, a man of indefatigable spirit and laser-like drive, decided he had had enough of conformity. The neighborhood he had been born into and on whose streets he had been raised was slowly dying of neglect, and Washington took it upon himself to forge a coalition of religious and civic leaders to lure the neighborhood back to life.

Fighting an uphill battle against an indifferent city hall, the antagonistic Reagan federal government, an anemic economy, and the endemic pessimism of the Bradhurst locals, Washington and his colleagues practiced resurrection by preaching hope. They bent the ears of their congregants and twisted the arms of their politicians. They fought for, cajoled, educed, and seduced every private and public dollar they could get their sights on so that they could at least get a shovel in the ground. Within three years they had a lot of shovels in the ground, and, as Washington pointed out, "We were digging foundations, not graves."

Because of their labors, Bradhurst was slowly but inexorably ascendant. Doors to over two thousand units of new and refurbished housing opened up to the community, and the vast majority of the units were tenant owned. (As one of Washington's aides dryly observed regarding home ownership, "No one ever washes a rented car.") After-school programs, computer-training tutorials, health-resource centers, nutrition classes, AIDS education activities, and for-profit commercial enterprises burgeoned. Every single construction contract was awarded to qualified, locally based, minority-run businesses. As unemployment plummeted income rose, and so did the spirits of those who, like Washington, had for so many years called this place their woe-begotten home.

Bradhurst was a neighborhood come back to life—*I who have died am alive again.* Marx was right to warn against religion as a tool of conformity that served the needs of the powerful to protect their power. Washington would not have disagreed, because by his reckoning the mandate of the church (synagogue, mosque, temple) is not to reflect cultural values, it is to critique, shape, and ultimately transform them. As Thomas Merton warned of a risk-averse faith that catered to the comfortable, "pseudo-goodness will prefer routine duty to courage and creativity. In the end it will be content with established procedures and safe formulas, while turning a blind eye to the greatest enormities of injustice and dishonesty." If we are to be a body that believes in the power of resurrection, that culls life out of death, that provides housing for the homeless, work for the unemployed, and dignity for the dispossessed, then we are not going to be content with safe formulas, because we will understand that in order for the seeds of justice to rise the structures that make for injustice must fall.

This understanding is not confined to politics or culture, but pervades the whole of our lives. After all, if a neighborhood can be resurrected, why not a family? As both a minister and a psychotherapist, I have seen time and "routine duty" slowly erode the affection between two long-ago lovers until seemingly nothing is left but the shallow comforts of that routine. I have also seen those lovers bring that relationship back to life, even when it has meant a new and different kind of life. I have seen siblings repair old wounds first inflicted years ago for reasons they no longer remember under circumstances they no longer agree upon and with justifications they no longer care about, where the only thing that seems to matter now is that the depth of their affection far outdistances the length of their estrangement.

Resurrection is the triumph of possibility over despair, but it is triumph only when we do the work to bring that possibility to life; think, for instance, of the work of Beethoven after he went completely deaf. Hearing is to a composer what hands are to a surgeon—the irreplaceable tools of his trade. But instead of letting his deafness sound the death knell to his life's calling, Beethoven, having declared "I will seize my fate by the throat!" seized his pen as well, put it to paper, and gave life to his most magnificent work, his magnum opus, his Ninth Symphony.

Resurrection is the work of creation and liberation, of embedded beauty freed from stone by the sculptor's hand, a woman freed from violence by dint of her own courage, or a tired neighborhood revived and revitalized by the preacher's will. It is the work of freedom fighters in Selma or Soweto or Stonewall who choose not to repay violence with violence. It is a genius who can hear the unspeakable beauty of a musical note when he can hear nothing else. It is even the stalk of corn that grows tall and defiant—if only in the hearts of the downtrodden—toward the summer's sun. Resurrection is what happens when the power to unite overcomes the power to divide, the power to create overcomes the power to destroy, the power of life overcomes the power of death.

Love Stronger Than Death

Finally, resurrection is perhaps the most pertinent of theological commentaries on God's love for us, because it presupposes death but also defies it, calls it out of that far-off corner of the room and dares it to spoil the party.

As God's emissary on earth—the human enactment of the divine intention—Jesus in his crucifixion reveals in human terms the limitless breadth of God's love for us. In the words of Paul, it is a love that was willing to be born in human likeness, and, "being found in human form, he humbled himself and became obedient to the point of death—even death on a cross" (Phil. 2:7–8). But that is only one piece of the equation, because if the crucifixion symbolizes the extent of God's love, the resurrection symbolizes its power. In Christ crucified we are freed from the weight of our sins, but in Christ resurrected we are freed from the weight of our fears that at death our relationship with the Divine dies with us. As Paul also wrote, "neither death, nor life, nor angels, nor rulers, nor powers, nor things present, nor things to come, nor height, nor depth, nor anything else in all creation, will be able to separate us from the love of God" (Rom. 8:38–39).

Scripture is as assertive about the reality of our relationship with God beyond this life as it is silent about its nature. It paints us no sentimental portraits of choirs of heavenly, haloed angels, no harps or lyres, no white robes, no pearly gates that frame a cloud-bedecked, cherub-guarded, and sun-drenched swath of celestial real estate. No, such is the stuff of low imagination peddled by primitive religionists who cannot abide the mystery. The Bible tells us nothing of the sort; it is too sublime a document to do so. What it does tell us is that on a sleepy Sunday morning many years ago the one who embodied the love of God made this promise to all who have eyes to see and ears to hear: that he who had died was alive again today on this gray, great, illimitable earth. That death could not hold him, any more than it can hold us. That a life well lived is one in which we are always dying creatively, always dying into life. It begins with our first breath, with which we die to the womb, and carries to our last, with which we die to the earth. It is then we discover that like the earth itself, God's love, too, is illimitable.

Questions for Discussion

Does one have to be a Christian to believe in the idea of resurrection?

What is the difference between Death and deaths? What do they have in common?

How do we "die creatively"? Can this term apply to the end of life?

What are some of the ways we can create life out of seemingly life-less situations?

Chapter 8

Reflection

I have spent my life seeking all that's still unsung. Bent my ears to hear the tune, and closed my eyes to see.

—The Grateful Dead

*I*t is commonly known as "the transfiguration," and we find it in the Gospel according to Matthew immediately after the disciple Peter has identified Jesus as the Christ and immediately before Jesus cures a little boy who suffered from epileptic seizures. As the story goes:

> Six days later, Jesus took with him Peter and James and his brother John and led them up a high mountain, by themselves. And he was transfigured before them, and his face shone like the sun, and his clothes became dazzling white. Suddenly there appeared with them Moses and Elijah, talking with him. Then Peter said to Jesus, "Lord, it is good for us to be here; if you wish, I will make three dwellings here, one for you, one for Moses, and one for Elijah." While he was still speaking, suddenly a bright cloud overshadowed them, and from the cloud a voice said, 'This is my Son, the Beloved; with him I am well pleased; listen to him!" When the disciples heard this, they fell to the ground and were overcome by fear. But Jesus came and touched them, saying, "Get up, and do not be afraid." And when they looked up, they saw no one except Jesus himself alone. (17:1–8)

To read this story for the first time is to be about as thunderstruck as the three disciples must have been. Feeding the multitude with a few loaves and fishes, as Jesus had done in the preceding chapter, was an impressive feat that now—compared to glowing light, glistening garments, the ghosts of Elijah and Moses, and the voice of God from a shimmering cloud—looks more like a cheap parlor trick than a miracle. But what do we make of it all?

The answer may be that there is no answer. Or, perhaps more to the point, there are several answers, depending upon which portal you choose to go through in order to enter the story. Look at it with the scholar's penchant for detached critique, and the first thing you may notice is the imagery of Jesus being united with two pillars of the past—Moses and Elijah—an interpolated literary device symbolizing the marriage of the Christ of the New Testament to the Law and the Prophets of the Old. On the other hand, look at it as the impassioned (and commissioned) sixteenth-century artist Raphael did, and you will see the dichotomy between Jesus' splendor and the disciples' confusion as reflecting the chasm between the sacred and the profane, the realm of celestial perfection set against the merely mortal.

Then again, imagine this story being read by a person of simple, elemental faith, who, on a cold night in a dark period of his life, is warmed by the blinding brilliance of the imagery, by the face of Christ that "shone like the sun," by the clothes "dazzling white," and by the bright cloud of God that overshadowed the disciples. He reads the words and recalls the crucial times in Scripture God appears as light—the burning bush that would not be consumed, the lightning on Mount Sinai, Paul's experience of "a light from heaven, brighter than the sun"—and how, in his aloneness and discouragement, he is comforted by this image. Perhaps he even recalls a time in his own life when things looked brighter, and as he thinks about this passage it takes him to those times, and he believes that they will come again, and all of this is good for his soul.

None of these interpretations is wrong, just as none of them is definitive. What they all are are *reflections*, musings, the subjectivity of personal experience meeting the objectivity of the revealed word. "To reflect" derives from *reflectere*, which means literally to "bend back" to where we were, as though taking a second look, a second, more studied chance for our eyes to see more deeply than they did at first glance. In experience we absorb the fact of an event, but in reflection we go back and discern its meaning; the one invites knowledge into our lives and the other transforms that knowledge into wisdom.

In ancient days the great rabbis mused on the question of how God spent his spare time, and more than a few of them weighed in with the proposition that he spent it studying Torah. Such was the esteem they attached to reflection and discernment that even God engaged in it. Centuries later a colleague of mine had a similar analogy when she observed, "I can analyze a rose for color and content. I can weigh and measure it. I can calculate its age, its density, and its rate of photosynthesis. But then," she added, "do I really *know* a rose?" The answer, of course, is yes. And no. She would know a rose the same way a rabbi who memorized the Torah would know the Torah. But in both cases it is only when the student asks of its subject not what it is but *what it means to them* that transformation begins to happen. Only then does the Torah become God's whisper and the rose God's beauty.

I believe this is at least in part what is behind the biblical notion of *imago dei*, the idea (that comes to us from Gen. 1:26) that human beings are made in God's image. It is in our power to think deeply, to find meaning within events and experiences, to discover the why behind the what, and from this to make wise and ethical decisions, that we are distinguished from "cattle and creeping things and wild animals of the earth" (Gen. 1:24) that God created before he deigned to breathe his spirit into us. As Clarence Darrow observes of humankind in *Inherit the Wind*, the elephant is mightier, the horse swifter, the gazelle more beautiful, the eagle far more majestic; but no animal has been given the gift of thought and reason to the extent that we have. Or, in Dante's words from *The Divine Comedy,* "Consider your origin; you were not born to live like brutes, but to follow virtue and knowledge."

To Bend Back for a Second Look

I do not know if God is poring over the Torah in his spare time, but we can take comfort in the belief that in study we ourselves are reflective, if not of God's image then at least of God's intent. The stories and lessons that Jesus (and other rabbis of his time) taught made his followers not only listen but think, and not just about the content of the story but about *what it meant to them*. Such is the power of studying and storytelling that we must dig beneath the surface in order to unearth the jewels.

When, for instance, we read yet again Psalm 23, we are touched by its poetry, but when we study it we learn that David wrote it on the occasion of the death of his son Absalom. With this as our backdrop we read of David's soul being restored, his walk through the shadowed valley, and the table prepared in the presence of his enemies in a very different, richer light, for it is now not just a proclamation of faith from the lips of a king—it is a reaffirmation of faith from the heart of a bereft father.

A similarly humbling moment of enlightenment came some years ago when I was on the staff of Riverside Church. Shortly after Nelson Mandela was released from prison after serving twenty-seven years for demanding freedom for black South Africans, he came to America. His first major public appearance was to be at a service in his honor in Riverside's great sanctuary. The event was going to be of monumental importance, but it was also a logistical nightmare, and, we were warned, the service could not run longer than the time given to it by television network coverage.

During the planning stages we met with the virtuoso West African drummer Babatunde Olatunji, whose elaborate drumbeat would bring Mandela into the sanctuary, up the aisle, and to his seat at the altar. Concerned about how long this might take and under pressure to keep things as simple as possible, I proposed to Baba that Mandela could come more quickly up the aisle with the rest of the procession, meet with the drums at the front of the sanctuary, and then be escorted to his seat. He smiled at me the way a grandparent might smile at an impertinent, impatient, and uneducated grandchild.

"My friend," he began, "I must tell you not what these drums are, but what they signify. In our culture, the job of the drums is to protect the king by driving away evil spirits. Those spirits might take any form, from spears cast by an avenging tribe to handcuffs wielded by the architects of apartheid. The king, at all costs, must be protected from evil, so it is the drummer's sacred responsibility, at the risk of his own life, to guide him, in every public appearance, from the time he enters until the time he is safely situated on his throne. To let him walk up the aisle without the drums is an affront to him and a breach of our custom. He protected us for twenty-seven years. We must now protect him. You do see, don't you?"

I not only saw, but when the event convened some weeks later and I watched Baba lead Mandela safely to his throne, I saw what to the uninitiated was an elaborate procession but to me, thanks to the tutelage of this great and patient sage, was now a gesture of profound reverence and binding love.

Olatunji's words were the light that was not meant to be kept under the bushel, because the insights we acquire through reflection can be personal but should not be kept private. They can be deeply meaningful to our lives, but we are incomplete with them if we fail to take to others the insights we have been afforded in our discipline as the *imago dei*. When he cast them upon me he threw a little light into a darkened place, and I was the better for it.

This is the beauty at the heart of the book of Deuteronomy. As Old Testament scholar Bonnie Kittel once observed, *Deutero nomia*, second law, can well be understood as "a second telling." It is less an extension of the tale of Israel's salvation than a recapitulation of the Hebrews' story. After a generation's worth of wilderness wandering, with all the miracles and misgivings that attended it, God has delivered the Hebrews to the edge of the promised land. It is here, in the story told twice, that the people reflect on where they have been and what they have learned so that they might put these thoughts to use in the place they are going. They are the reflections that will illuminate their path to freedom, the drumbeat effort to keep the evils at bay. In this way Deuteronomy's author shows us that reflection is more than the accumulation of wisdom, it is also the imparting of love.

Introspection and Courage

But wisdom gleaned from another's observations comes easily compared to those that are homegrown. Some years ago I worked with a patient by the name of Philip, himself a virtuous sort. In his early forties, Philip had worked hard to rise high in the ranks of a major multinational corporation and found great meaning in his chosen field. He had a strong marriage, three kids he doted on, and an enviable social life. Philip was by every measure a successful man. But he came to therapy nonetheless, as many people do, complaining of nonspecific miseries that eventually steered him back to conversations of his youth. In particular, Philip locked in on the ambiguities of his relationship to a father who was a good provider but whose own insecurities often surfaced in insidious and hurtful ways. Philip's dad could be quite mercurial; he was generous to a fault one minute and a real bully the next. He was a family man who knocked himself out to attend as many of his kid's athletic events as he could, but he was also an adulterer. He made good money but always tried to live as though he made better.

After some months spent dissecting this relationship Philip came to a crossroads that he defined thusly: "I can see how a lot of my unhealthier impulses are grounded in a desire to please my dad, and by my reckoning I can do one of three things with that. I can hate him for laying his insecurities on me, I can hate myself for continuing to buy into his game, or I can decide that he doesn't have to have that power over me." Suffice it to say he chose wisely.

It was not all that long after this that Philip's dad died suddenly, and in his session immediately following the funeral he was anxious to share with me the eulogy he delivered. It was a kind, forgiving, but honest piece of prose in which the son was able to define the father's foibles with equal measures of grace and judgment. There was much to be admired in the man, as well as much to be forgiven, and Philip did both. When I asked him what the whole of the experience had left him with he put it this way: "It was good for me to reflect on the totality of my dad, to see him from some distance, because it showed me a guy who, in the end, was by no means perfect but was simply doing the best he could with what he had. I'm very much at peace with that." Philip's peace was earned and paid for by the work of reflection, of bending back to take a broader, more illuminated look, a look that did not so much transfigure his father as transform Philip's understanding of him.

I was as impressed by Philip's insights as by the courage it took for him to arrive at them. At times reflection requires courage because it can be an unnerving proposition when it means giving up cherished truths, and this is what he had to do when he decided to let his father off the hook for the years of grief the old man had saddled his son with. When we bend back for that second look we may see mistakes we did not know we had made, or we may find that easy answers are supplanted by hard questions that leave us with that age-old realization that the more we learn the less we know. As Shakespeare said in *As You Like It,* "The fool doth think himself wise, but the wise man knows himself to be a fool."

Thus God's goodness was an easy nugget for the upright Job to digest when in his prosperity he was "the greatest of all the people of the east" (1:3), but it was a lot tougher to swallow when calamity beset him, and he lost all he had, including belief in a God who treated him as justly as he treated that God. The truth is, we all have our Job moments.

Some years ago when (as I mention in an earlier chapter) our then fourteen-year-old daughter was seriously injured in an automobile accident—our family's Job moment—many people asked me if my trust in God had been shaken by her injuries or buttressed by her recovery. In my own time of reflection I came to realize that neither may have been the case, that my prayers for her were rooted more in desperation than faith, that I did not believe in a God who arbitrarily protects one child while letting others die, and that if God *was* the final arbiter of her recovery I would never understand the logic behind it. The whole experience neither rattled nor resolved my faith, but it subtly altered it, because any pronouncements I once made about the terrible and wonderful things that can happen in this world, pronouncements that had once been little more than well-reasoned observations made at arm's-length safety, were now grounded in the rock-hard reality of my own experience. I have no choice but to believe that God is with me, just as I have no choice but to believe that, like Job, or Philip, or the reader of these words, that neither delivers me to unmerited pleasures nor insulates me from undeserved pains.

The Beginning of Wisdom

Reflection does not make us safer but it does make us wiser, and that in turn can make us better. Reflection allowed me to better comprehend the reverence with which so many Africans held Nelson Mandela, made Philip hold his father in higher esteem, perhaps even made the God of the ancient rabbis better understand the elegance of his own law code. But it must be more a discipline than an occasional glance, more a part of life than a momentary awareness.

One night, not long after 9/11, a professional football player was being interviewed on the news. He was asked how the events of that day would affect the players and their upcoming season. "You know," he began, "something like this really puts things in perspective for us as Americans. It reminds me that what I do for a living, as much as we're idolized, is really pretty unimportant. Fact is, I'm paid a large sum of money to play a child's game, and the real heroes are the folks who lay their lives on the line every day for us—the cops, the fire-fighters, the medics. It's time guys like us [athletes] appreciate guys like them."

This man's sentiments were echoed in one form or another by a good many people throughout the coming weeks; there was a lot of brotherhood and sisterhood in the air, a lot of effort put forth to put things in perspective, take stock of what really matters in life and what is mere window dressing. But as much as the athlete's words had heart, they lacked legs.

Before long, pros like he were again demanding more millions to play their child's game or explaining to the beat reporters that they had no idea how the cocaine found its way into their glove compartment or how they found their way into the strip club. Strangers who once embraced in a spirit of shared grief and newfound patriotism were again reduced to fighting over a theater seat or a dry cleaning bill. Statesmen squandered unprecedented international goodwill by initiating a war that satisfied their thirst for vengeance but left unmet our need for justice. A great many of us, pledging to get back to caring about what *really* mattered in life, did so for a while but eventually got back to caring about whether Britney would go to rehab or Paris to jail, or whether the owner of our favorite team would overlook the drug bust and meet the contract demands of our star running back or center fielder or point guard.

It is one thing to put things in perspective, as the football player said. It is quite another to keep them there. If we are to be better for having reflected on what is important in life, it will be because when we explore our lives we will do so with more an honest examination than a cursory glance. When we read our Scriptures we will accept the uncomfortable truths they reveal about discipleship's costs just as we accept the comforting truths they reveal about its joys. Our prayers of thanks will be offered with the same passion as our prayers of petition.

In the great swirl of paradox and contradiction in which life is so often embedded, reflection will not make life easier but it will make it more lucid, because this is what wisdom offers us, even in small doses. "Lucidity" is from the Latin *lucidus*, "light." We will see better. God willing, we will shine that light in darkened places where we love too little or judge too much. Through reflection we will learn to minimize our sins of selfishness or self-pity, our anxieties over bad things that never happen, our priorities that value popular choices over principled ones. We will learn when stubbornness is good but also when flexibility is better, and how compromise can be a tactic without being either a capitulation or a manipulation. We will distinguish between needs and wants, appreciating the former and moderating the latter. In coming to know how much we do not know, how much lies beyond our comprehension, we will learn how thoroughly dependent we are on others, and in that dependency we will become both more compassionate toward our fellow human beings and more appreciative of them.

An old friend once told me the story of his moment of reflective awareness on the 5:18 commuter train from New Haven to New York City. He had been born to privilege and lived well but always worked as an advocate for the poor and powerless.

"I was gazing out the window of the train," he told me, "looking at the elegant homes we passed by in the city's tonier suburbs. It was quite relaxing.

"Then, getting closer to Grand Central, we're suddenly in a very, very poor part of the Bronx. Buildings with no windows, but with clotheslines stretched across indicating that people lived there. Bricks coming loose. Doors off their hinges. Real rough stuff. It broke my heart to see, especially when I saw young kids coming and going out the front doors.

"Then, just as suddenly, as we're approaching Manhattan, the train enters a tunnel. Where just a moment ago I was looking at abject poverty I am now in a darkened cave, with the interior lights from the train car the only illumination. Now, as I stare out the window, *all I see is my own reflection.* I tell you it was a clarion call. It shook me to my well-shined shoes. And it told me that I cannot separate myself from the people I saw and the conditions they find themselves in. We are of one flesh."

For my friend it was literally his reflection that put things in perspective for him, and I believe he kept that perspective. He lived a life of material simplicity, continued his efforts as a preacher and a writer on behalf of the maligned of the world, and, whenever he rode the New Haven line, he saw to it that he had the window seat that looked outward to the Bronx, and inward to his own salvation. He shined a light into a dark place, and he found people from whom he could not separate himself.

Of course the fruits of reflection more often come to us in less dramatic ways, the product of study and quiet thought, of introspection and observation, the slow and solitary process of divining God's hand in our world, of knowing, in the words of the old balladeer Leonard Cohen, "where to look amid the garbage and the flowers," and perhaps finding God's hand in both.

When I reflect upon the transfiguration I am, like the disciples, in awe and fear. But these are fleeting feelings, and I am more at home with the metaphor of light that suffuses the story. There is something more modest about this, but also more enduring. I think less of a blinding flash from the heavens than I do a steady candle in the dead of night, which, in the end, is what Jesus asked his followers to be. He was not normally prone to great theatrics or displays of power, and perhaps this is why he brought only two of his own to witness the event. He did not want this to be central to their way of thinking. Instead, I believe he wanted them to reflect upon it themselves, be themselves illumined by what they saw, and, like a kid chasing a lightning bug, grab a little of the magic, and glow.

So it is that I am less prone to be stirred to the kind of grand vision that took hold of Raphael by this extraordinary moment in faith history than drawn back to the words from an old African American hymn that warms my soul by its gently spirited lyrics:

Some say the time's not right,
But we say the time's just right!
If there's a dark corner in our land,
You got to let your little light shine.
This little light of mine,
I'm gonna let it shine,
Let it shine, let it shine, let it shine.

Let it shine. From the campfire around which Moses gathered his people to ponder their fate, let it shine. From the chandeliered ceiling of a great American cathedral where once strode Africa's reluctant, triumphant leader, let it shine. From the glowing eulogy of a son for his father or the melancholic psalm of a father for his son, let it shine. From the fluorescent bulbs of the 5:18 out of New Haven, let it shine. We cannot create divine light. That is not our purpose. But we can reflect it. That most certainly *is* our purpose.

Questions for Discussion

How can temporal distance from an event—a separation of time—help us to better understand the meaning of the event? Have you had such an experience?

What is the difference in our lives between knowledge and wisdom? How does each serve us?

How can the act of study be a religious act, even if it is not religion per se that we are studying?

Chapter 9

Religion

Bart [Simpson], we're here to bring you back to the one true faith: The Western branch of American Reformed Presbylutheranism.

— Pastor Timothy Lovejoy, *The Simpsons*

*T*hree thoughts worthy of consideration:

One: "Six days shall work be done, but the seventh day is a sabbath of solemn rest, holy to the LORD; whoever does any work on the sabbath day shall be put to death."

Two: "I really believe that the pagans and the abortionists, and the feminists, and the gays and the lesbians . . . and the ACLU, People for the American Way, all of them have tried to secularize America. I point the finger in their faces and say, 'You helped [9/11] happen!'"

Three: "Three passions, simple but overwhelmingly strong, have governed my life: the longing for love, the search for knowledge, and unbearable pity for the suffering of mankind."

The first quotation is from the book of Exodus (31:15); the second from the late, self-appointed arbiter of American morality, Jerry Falwell; and the third from Bertrand Russell, twentieth-century philosopher, mathematician, pacifist, and inveterate nonbeliever. If I had to choose one of the three as a foundation on which to build a new society, I would go with Russell in a heartbeat. Herein lies the problem that religion faces today, wounded by its own words, some self-inflicted and some the product of lazy thinking or sloppy analysis on the part of its critics: It has come to be identified with anti-intellectualism,

95

bigotry, extremism, intolerance, and hypocrisy. In some circles it is seen as irrelevant to the question of the origin of ethics, and in others it is an impediment to their evolution. When religion's critics are generous they dismiss religion as benign, but when they are harsh they label it dangerous, and their criticisms are not necessarily without merit. As one observer noted with regard to religious extremism, "Did you ever notice that we never seem to hear about atheist terrorists?"

But it is not that simple, because nothing is. When Gandhi was once asked what he thought of civilization, he responded, "It seems like a good idea," and the same can be said for religion. It is a fundamentally good idea that has in many ways become so obscured as to be barely recognizable. But we do not need to get rid of it, any more than we need to get rid of civilization. To the contrary, we need to get it back.

A Wolf in Sheep's Clothing

For anyone who wants to be a critic of religion in this day and age the greatest challenge might be deciding on which front to launch an assault. Perhaps one can start with the biblical literalists, who apply a tortured kind of pseudoscience to stories like the creation, the ten plagues of Pharaoh, or Daniel in the lion's den because they are so invested in the historicity of the events that they fail to see their subtler truths, their metaphors, and their intrinsic beauties. Or if not them then perhaps the Christian supremacists make a good target, the fearmongers who reject the authenticity of any faith other than their own, who proclaim the United States the new Israel, whose Cassandra call foresees only mortal trouble across the United States unless each and every one of us accepts their version of Jesus as our own.

But if not these low-hanging fruits, there are always the high-flying hypocrites, the ones who preach modesty, chastity, and austerity before getting caught with their hand in the cookie jar, their photograph at a seedy motel, or their name on a large check from a disgraced lobbyist or lawmaker. It is only then that they seem to remember confession and forgiveness are part of the religious equation as well. Or if not the hypocrites, the celebrity faddists who become overnight devotees of some bronzed Hollywood shaman because he promises inner peace and endless prosperity if only they will endorse his CDs with titles like *The Inner Winner* or *Why God Wants You to Be Rich*, or land him on the cover of *People* magazine.

Beyond these caricatures there are the less insidious, more immediate threats, the extremist who would assassinate Mahatma Gandhi in the name of Ishvara, fly a plane into a building in the name of Allah, lob a hand grenade into a Palestinian refugee camp in the name of Yhwh, or shoot an abortion provider to death at point-blank range in the name of Jesus. When false certainty is construed from religious stridency, the outcome of even the most heinous act is sanctified by the warped logic of the one who is committing it.

But to excoriate all religion because of the excesses of some religious people is itself an act of extremism and intolerance. There is another side to the coin.

The Courage of Conviction

There is a well-known saying from the late bishop of Brazil, Dom Helder Camara, who, when asked about his commitment to social justice, answered, "When I give food to the poor they call me a saint. When I ask why the poor have no food they call me a communist." Religion at its best does both; it tends to the poor while simultaneously challenging the social and political structures that abide their poverty. This is why we find soup kitchens and food drives in houses of worship but why you also find foundations like the Roman Catholic charity Bread for the World and the Chicago-based Council for Islamic Organizations lobbying Congress on behalf of anti-hunger legislation. Religion is the good Samaritan tending to the victim on the road, but it is also the squeaky-wheeled irritant demanding to know why the government has not made that road safer.

Religious communities as almsgivers and advocates are as inextricably entwined with the American scene as baseball and barbecues. It was these communities that led and sometimes initiated the American abolitionist movement, the civil rights movement, and the suffragists. Religious visionaries cofounded the nuclear disarmament campaign, César Chávez's United Farm Workers, and Clergy and Laity Concerned about Vietnam (CALCAV). They launched, funded, and to this day sustain the Interfaith Center for Corporate Responsibility, the American Friends Service Committee, and the Religious Campaign Against the Death Penalty. It has long been said that the prophet is the one who speaks the greatest truth where it is the least welcomed, and religious prophets of all faiths and creeds have, over the years, refused to be silenced in the face of the most unwelcomed truths.

It was the Stephen Wise Synagogue in New York City that, in 2006, launched the nationwide campaign to end the silence over the atrocities in Darfur, just as it had been the Anglican Church thirty years earlier that began calling attention to the atrocities of South African apartheid. The United Church of Christ spends over $4 million annually on peace and justice ministries, the Islamic Society of North America spends over $6 million, and no community has a more consistent track record when it comes to dedicating themselves to a peaceful life in a warring world than the Quakers. When refugees have needed resettlement in Bosnia or hurricane victims have needed homes in New Orleans, the religious communities delivered it for them. When potable water was needed in a distant Malawian village or malaria shots in an Appalachian holler, they delivered there as well. When elderly have needed hospice care or infants have needed pro bono reconstructive surgery, there too have religious communities made good on their word to serve humankind. Without hesitation or fanfare, with no attention to race or nationality or faith affiliation, all the great religions have, both historically and to this day, sought to bring a little heaven to hellish places. And they have done so with luminous humility, gratitude, and grace.

God, Faith, and Humanity

For those of us who believe in the premise that God—by whatever name—exists, we need religion, because it is not enough to have a seed without the soil. We need a place to explore and enlarge on that premise, a place where belief can mature into relationship, a community in which we can have our assumptions challenged, our horizons broadened, our trust substantiated. It is not always a neat fit, this relationship. It is prone to quarrels, slights, and misgivings. There are times when our religion fails us and other times when we fail it. But without it, without a sacred text, a fellowship, and a liturgy that together articulate an (admittedly) imperfect understanding of an otherwise unknowable God, we are essentially alone with this God, a student with no teacher, a celebrant with no song, a pilgrim with not so much as a trail of bread crumbs to help us find our way home. To paraphrase the nineteenth-century novelist Christopher Morley, religion is a noble attempt to express in human terms more-than-human realities.

Scripture

In the beginning is the word. The spine of every modern religion is the collection of stories contained in its sacred texts. In the recounting of history through a lens of faith—whether the vehicle be myth, legend, poetry, or chronicle—the reader is introduced less to God than to how God has been perceived and experienced by the tellers of the tales. To say that God is love, or judgment, or wisdom is to say that this faith community has experienced what they call love, judgment, or wisdom from God and have imparted it here in these writings. The word *religion* is itself derived from the Latin *relegere,* meaning "to read again," and suggests it is at God's direction that we return to these texts in order that we might see our own experience of God reflected in those of our forebears.

Our relationship to Scripture, like our relationship to religion, is not always a comfortable one. We are often wrestling with the meaning of tales first told thousands of years ago around councils, committees, or campfires by people with their own agendas to advance. The stories have been embellished by the teller, buffed and clipped, edited to suit the bias of this or that community, often without regard for consistency (did Noah take two of every animal onto the ark, as written in Gen. 6:19, or seven of every animal, as written in 7:2?).

They give us abundant detail on how to manage a herd dispute between nomadic tribes or the proper way to clean up after the slaughter of a sacrificial goat, but are of course silent on the question of whether the use of stem cells is a morally justifiable way to save lives or the use of nuclear weapons is a morally justifiable way to take them.

All this is to say they must be approached with great care and respect, trusting that the text is willing to give up its secrets to the person who is willing to discern them. There is an element of the artistic to them. When we look at a work of Jackson Pollock, such as his cacophonous *Lavender Mist,* we can either reduce it to a riot of squiggles and smears "that any six-year-old could do," or we can appreciate it as a product of genius, absorb ourselves in it, discover the undercurrent of order beneath the surface chaos, note the eagerness with which our eyes move from place to place across the huge canvas, and therein feel something of the artist's congenital and ultimately fatal restlessness. In other words, we can ask the painting to do the heavy lifting for us or we can engage it, question it, mine it, and uncover its treasures.

This is why holy writ from any religious heritage is cheapened by those who—armed with nothing more than a conclusion in search of a hypothesis—take scriptural snippets out of context and hold them up as divine validation for whatever point they are trying to make. Does the Bible condone war or condemn it? Read the book of Joshua, where the author writes, "about forty thousand ready armed for war crossed over before the LORD to the plains of Jericho for battle. On that day the LORD exalted Joshua in the sight of all Israel" (4:13–14); or Exodus, where we read, "A hand upon the banner of the LORD! The LORD will have war with Amalek from generation to generation" (17:16), and you get hearty grist for the warrior's mill. On the other hand Joel enjoins the faithful to "beat their swords into plowshares, and their spears into pruning hooks" (3:10), 1 Peter, quoting Psalm 34, bids us to "seek peace and pursue it" (3:11), and Jesus himself reminds his followers, "Blessed are the peacemakers, for they shall be called children of God" (Matt. 5:9).

So what *does* the Bible say about war? The faithful will disagree on this question, as we always have, and as we will on innumerable other questions of behavior and belief, from capital punishment to infant baptism to the divinity of Mary. But better honest disagreement in search of a difficult truth than cheap rhetorical sleights of hand in search of an easy one. We owe the text at least this much.

Community

We do not take on those hard questions alone; we take them on with others, and we do so because the religious life, like life itself, is not lived in total isolation. Even the hermit monks and ancient mystics were members of brotherhoods who saw their solitude as both feeding on and contributing to the greater good of a wider community.

It is into the religious fellowship that we are born, baptized, and bat mitzvahed. As young children we squirm our way through services, draw crayon pictures of the garden of Eden, and tell our parents all we have learned in Sunday school about how God is bigger than big. Unbeknownst to us, it is our first taste of that community. Later we may go off to church camp, where, in the words of the Old Testament scholar Brevard Childs, "We get Jesus, mosquito bites, and, if we're lucky, our first kiss." Counselors sneak religion to us through the back door, with late-night conversations about things like sexual ethics and human values, because they know that at this age religion and cool do not mix, and cool is very, very important.

Later still, some of us are unsettled by questions that seem greater than our religion's ability to answer them. Somebody young dies, a parent leaves home, or a terrible earthquake kills thousands of innocent people in a faraway land. Or perhaps nothing of any great import happens, but religion has come to feel as bland and tepid to us as our college civics class—inoffensive, but tedious and hardly worth our time. So we drift away from that community, perhaps sniff around to see if there is more excitement to be found elsewhere, in other modes of seeking, or perhaps not.

Then somewhere along the line, for some of us, circumstances conspire to return us to religion, and whether it is to the religion of our childhood or another we are still welcomed by the community and grateful to be part of it. We get a second chance. At times contentious, at times petty, always a learning process, the community is also a devoted, active expression of the faith we want so much to find again in our lives. Common creed brings us to identify with one another, which brings us to appreciate and understand one another, which in turn brings us to care for one another. In this way, we are family—people who often but not always like one another but who always aspire to love one another, if for no other reason than because this love is at the very heart of that creed we commonly claim as our own.

It is family because these are the people with whom we admit our fears, our misgivings, and our misdeeds, and who can hear that admission without need for query or explanation. It is here that we allow our doubts to surface because we know that they will be met with both wisdom and generosity by people for whom doubt is also no stranger, that our words are not foreign to the sensibility of the other. These are the people who know when we are ill and pray for our recovery, know when life has been good to us and celebrate our triumphs, know when we have suffered loss and weep with us the anguished tears of bitter grief. They are our fellowship to whom we are attached by shared belief, which is no small attachment.

Liturgy

Sitting in a church does not make us a Christian any more than sitting in a garage makes us a mechanic, but it is in liturgy that our religion brings that fellowship together and coheres for us. Worship is our watering hole, our town square. It is the time and place in which we gather from distant walks to be of one voice. To paraphrase Paul, here we are neither male nor female nor slave nor free, nor Republican nor Democrat, nor college professor nor street sweeper, nor able-bodied nor wheelchair-bound, nor old nor young, nor black nor white nor yellow nor red nor brown. Here in this place, in this hour, God's devotion to us and ours to God supersedes all differences of birth, chance, choice, or affiliation.

I remember the first time I heard a live presentation of an extraordinary piece of sacred music called "Teranga," composed and performed by the eminent jazz trumpeter Jon Faddis. It is a piece that captures this sense of unity without having to cudgel us with it. As Faddis explains, *teranga* is a Senegalese word that roughly translates as "hospitality," but more than this it stands for a strong moral obligation to welcome strangers into our community with the understanding that such kindness on our part not only benefits the stranger but benefits us and our children as well. The piece is slight and quiet at the outset, a timid flute lost like a stranger among the pulsing drums, slowly feeling its way into the music as the other instruments—the existing fellowship—come into play. The pace quickens and grows richer, the flute cautiously finding its voice as though it is not yet certain it belongs here but is beginning to feel its welcome. Then, like a tribal elder greeting a weary wanderer, Faddis's trumpet overrides the beat but still leaves us room for the flute to be heard. Before long, as all the instruments blend into one exquisite sound, we realize that we have been liturgically lifted above the disparateness that can keep us at arm's length from one another, each instrument thoroughly dependent upon the other to make the sound as rich as it is. At this point there are no strangers, there is just pure hospitality. To hear it is to be in God's space.

Perhaps that space is at the feet of a jazz impresario or perhaps not. Perhaps it is in a modest clapboard church of the western Great Plains or one of the majestically spired cathedrals of Dallas, Texas. Or maybe it is in the squat little immigrants' synagogue of New York City's Lower East Side, with its peeling paint and pitted façade, the one that now provides counterpoint to the chic cafés and high-priced boutiques that surround it. Or if not there perhaps it is the call to prayer heard above the clatter of the El from one of the onion-domed mosques in Chicago's South Side. Whatever the house of prayer, whether we are called to it by the rabbi's shofar, the priest's pealing bells, the imam's *adhan* (the Islamic call to prayer), or the jazzman's high C, we gratefully heed it. By week's end we are ready to be with one another again, to feel the sun streaming in through stained glass, to sing the hymns of our youth, and, if they must, to let subdued emotions find their voice and be totally unashamed. When we are here we are free to use language we rarely use in public the other days of the week. It is here that we feel as though we have slipped into the waiting arms of God, and here we remove ourselves from the world but only so that we might be better prepared to return to it. For this is why we worship, because in the moment it is a good experience and beyond the moment it is a sustaining one, our weekly second chance. Or, in the inspiring words of Alfred North Whitehead, "The worship of God is not a rule of safety—it is an adventure of the spirit, and flight after the unattainable."

Hubris and Humility

Our relationship to religion is sometimes like that of à kid to a chemistry lab: all the ingredients are there for good things to happen, but if they are not used wisely, chaos can ensue. Scripture is sublime but fragile and easily mishandled—even Hitler quoted it. Worship can be as dulcet and transfixing as a wonderful symphony. But it can also resemble a terrible one, a smattering of noise that does not justify itself with purpose or beauty. Doctrine that is meant to codify religious beliefs can also calcify them, just as, at the other extreme, liberalism can morph into relativism.

For all these foibles nothing makes that chemistry more deadly than an ill-reasoned and unmerited religious superiority complex, and this is where the chemicals can mix in a very bad way. When I think of the offenses committed in my lifetime alone in the name of religion, I am most appalled at what comes of religious conceit, which I define as misplaced certainty disguised as heartfelt conviction to disastrous effect.

One example of an offense comes out of Afghanistan, where shortly after the Taliban came to power their religious leadership decided that two great stone statues of Buddha perched up in the hillsides in the Afghani town of Bamiyan (second-century relics standing over fifty meters high) were an affront to Islam. Rejecting appeals from all over the world, including those from Islamic scholars and clergy, to allow the statues to be relocated to Thailand, the Taliban instead fired upon them with rocket mortars and dynamite, reducing them to dust. This was not an act of reverence for their own beliefs; it was an act of intolerance for the beliefs of others.

In another hemisphere, the verbal dynamite that comes flying out of the mouths of some so-called religious leaders in the United States may not fell relics but can chill discussion about religious pluralism and leave others wondering how safe they should feel in a nation where 85 percent of us claim to be Christian. When from James Dobson's Family Research Council I read, "While it is true that the United States of America was founded on the sacred principle of religious freedom for all, that liberty was never intended to exalt other religions to the level that Christianity holds in our country's heritage," I can only imagine how this sentiment must sit with, say, the Sikhs, Jews, Muslims, Baha'i, Zoroastrians, or Hindus who call the United States their home.

Dobson's statement is a not-so-subtle dig at all religions not based on the teachings of Christ but not nearly as blunt as the words of Bailey Smith, a founder of Pat Robertson's Christian Coalition, who, at a religious roundtable in 1994, opined: "With all due respect to these dear people, my friend, God Almighty does not hear the prayer of a Jew."

On the other hand, with this kind of arrogance born of ignorance coming out of the mouths of national opinion shapers I am heartened to read one religious leader's more modest observation, "the more I learn the less dogmatic I become," especially when that leader's name is Billy Graham. As Graham went on to say in the same conversation, "I used to believe that pagans in far-off countries were lost—were going to hell—if they did not have the gospel of Jesus Christ preached to them. I no longer believe that." Confession is always good for the soul, and wisdom always attenuates dogma.

It is not Christianity that is to blame for the screeds of the supremacists any more than Islam should be held accountable for the excesses of the Taliban, Hinduism for discrimination against Indian Muslims, or Judaism for the humiliating checkpoints Palestinians must pass through in Israel. It is not religion but the perversion of religion by those who think they have cornered the market on truth that is the real culprit here: the kid in the chem lab who is sure he knows it all and will brook no dissent from anyone who thinks otherwise, even long after his words have blown up in his face. One does not hold the test tubes responsible.

Graham's humility is encouraging because after preaching for so many years that Jesus provided the only means to human salvation, he came to comprehend that God and God's will cannot be limited by the definitions we humans (including himself) put on God. They are *our* constructs, not God's. More often than not they are honestly come by and deeply held, but they are also influenced by time, place, and the inscrutability of our own subconscious prejudices. What Graham did was religious in its truest sense—he went back to the word, where sometimes the greatest wisdom we can glean is an appreciation of how much of it we still do not fully understand.

Whither the Faith

For any religion to be a force for good in the twenty-first century it cannot cloak itself in indefensible certainties that contradict the indefensible certainties of other religions. Nor, on the other hand, is there good to be found in tacking in the other direction, where, as the old joke has it, the Ten Commandments become the Ten Suggestions. In the drift away from dogmatic certainty, the risk is for a church (or mosque, or synagogue, or temple) to offer a kind of mall religion: a least-common-denominator, one-size-fits-all street fair that aims to please everybody and offend nobody, a place where comfort is the creed and axioms like "feel good about yourself" supplant old downers like "whatever you have done for the least of my brothers or sisters, you have done for me." Bill McKibben put it this way in regard to the so-called megachurch movement:

> A *New York Times* reporter visiting one booming megachurch outside Phoenix recently found the typical scene: a drive-through latte stand, Krispy Kreme doughnuts at every service, and sermons about "how to discipline your children, how to reach your professional goals, how to invest your money, how to reduce your debt." On Sunday children played with church-distributed Xboxes, and many congregants had signed up for a twice-weekly aerobics class called Firm Believers.
>
> *Harper's*, August 2005

As McKibben mentions later in the piece, these things are not so bad in themselves, but do they make for a *church*?

As a Christian I can only proclaim that in the person of Jesus I have met *my* Christ, *my* savior, *my* gateway to God. I am certain of my proclamation, just as I am certain that that same God offers other gateways to other pilgrims as well; as George Bernard Shaw put it, "There is only one religion, though there are a hundred versions of it." Of these, be they at all similar to my way or barely recognizable to me, all I can ask is that the God we meet deepens our passion for life, reminds us of the limits of our own wisdom, and helps us to look with compassion on our fellow human beings. Or, in the words of one very wise man who decided to go it alone (his loss), may our religion stir in us nothing less than "the longing for love, the search for knowledge, and unbearable pity for the suffering of mankind."

Questions for Discussion

How do we distinguish between religion and faith? Can we embrace one but not the other?

Do we have a responsibility to critique our religion? If so, how best do we do this?

Why do religions sometimes drift far afield of their principles, and what can we do about that?

How can our religion serve us in ways that no other communions or institutions can?

Chapter 10

Receiving

To be empty is to be full.

—Lao Tzu

Finding Clarity amid the Clutter

On a sunny summer afternoon back in the mid-70s Josh Waitzkin, a New York City kid who thought he was a pretty unremarkable six-year-old, discovered that he was not. While strolling through Washington Square Park with his mom, Josh decided to forego the seesaw and swing set and instead try to play chess. He had never played the game before, but Josh beat all comers—players three and four times his age—and four years later, at the age of ten, he defeated his first master. Recognizing that he had a rare gift, when he was nine Josh's parents hired a renowned chess coach, a taskmaster by the name of Bruce Pandolfini, to hone Josh's skills.

One evening late into a lesson Pandolfini arranged the chess board with about six or seven pieces, the whites arrayed in a seemingly impenetrable defense of the king. "Do you see the weakness?" he asked, but Josh did not. "Look harder," he ordered repeatedly, sometimes with patience, sometimes with barely stifled rage. But Josh could not see the opening.

In what was either a fit of pique or a stroke of brilliance, Pandolfini suddenly, violently, swiped his arm across the table, sending the pieces skittering wildly, bouncing off walls, ricocheting off furniture.

Now with the empty board staring back at them, the master again asked the boy, quietly, "What about now?"

Josh paused for a moment, then exclaimed, "Aha! Yes. Now I see it!"

What I treasure about this story is that it serves as a theological metaphor for what we must do before we can see the evident mystery of divine love, the invisible that sits right in front of our eyes. The only way to find what is hidden in plain sight is to clear our minds of all clutter and assumptions.

In God's framework we are not loved because we are handsome, nor are we handsome because we are loved. We do not win God's favor with clever jokes or parlor tricks. And beware the Rolex and Rolls Royce TV preacher, the one Jeremiah Wright bluntly calls the "prosperity pimp," who tells us that the measure of God's affection is proportionate to our contribution to his ministry. It is not, nor can God's love be measured by the kindest of deeds done with the purest of intentions to the greatest effects. Divine love is neither measured nor meted out nor earned. It is simply bestowed, unsparingly, so much so that, in the words of the Song of Solomon, "Many waters cannot quench love, neither can floods drown it" (8:7).

Our inability to buy our way into God's favor is why priests offer prayers of supplication and invitation with their arms opened and their hands empty. The gesture replicates our symbolic poverty, the emptiness from which we ask for and receive the love that is God's grace. We hold no coin, they are telling us, and cannot buy what is free. We are loved by virtue of our being, not our doing. This is what is behind what Jesus teaches his followers in the Gospel of Matthew: "everyone who has left houses or brothers or sisters or father or mother or children or fields, for my name's sake, will receive a hundredfold, and will inherit eternal life" (19:29). He is assuring them that to empty themselves, to leave all other sureties behind, is to put themselves in a position to receive the love he is offering. They can see what is left, and it is pure. It is their "Aha!" moment.

But discovering the fact of God's love is not the same as discerning its meaning, and meaning is everything. To Einstein the splitting of the atom was the birth of a new era of scientific inquiry; to Edward Teller it was the birth of the nuclear bomb. The question we must ask ourselves is not whether God loves us, but how we are to receive this love and what we are to do with it.

Poverty as the Disposition of Receiving

There is no better metaphor for what it means to receive divine love without condition or contract than a newborn baby. She is the quintessence of poverty, this child, an empty receptacle, thoroughly vulnerable, powerless to care for herself beyond her ability to draw a breath. She has no assets to barter what she needs, no ego to get in the way of her acknowledging those needs, and no guile at her disposal to manipulate how she gets them met. She is totally and utterly at the mercy of the angels whose job it is to care for her.

But as she begins to grow, things change. She learns to do for herself, to hold a spoon, to tie a shoelace. She draws a bit distant from her angels, and receiving is no longer a measure of helplessness.

A little later, she learns that with the slightest manipulation—an endearing if contrived smile, an embellished sadness, a raging tantrum—she can get those angels to give to her what they otherwise might not. Her receiving is now not quite as pure as it once was.

Later still, as self-consciousness begins to replace her unbridled sincerity, she becomes reticent about giving voice to what she needs. She is unsure about telling the teacher she requires help with her math, or asking a friend to go with her to the dance. She is more concerned with how others will see her than how she really is, and so she sublimates what is deep inside her, and her needs go unmet. This is the first sign of the debilitating side of pride, the side that makes it harder for her to reach out for fear that in receiving something small she may be giving up something great.

Our relationship with God can follow a similar path. Over time, we easily forget that our lives are not merited but bestowed, and that we exist only because God calls us into existence. We forget that we cannot earn our way into God's grace any more than we can sin our way out of it. We also forget that in order to receive that grace we must acknowledge that we need it, that we are not complete without it, that *our* pride can only serve to keep us from it. We must be like the newborn, devoid of pride, fully needy, open to receive the love of the divine parent.

Receiving God's love means understanding that it comes to us unconditionally, the rain that falls on the just and unjust alike. In Jericho it came to the good Samaritan, but also to the man he rescued on the side of the road, the priest who passed him by, and the thieves who robbed him. In Jerusalem it came to Mary, who had given Jesus life, and to Judas, who ensured his death. In Dachau it came to the prisoners, to those who imprisoned them, and to those who risked their own lives to liberate them. Sometimes we know how to receive this love, the way a darkened room receives the light of day, while other times we simply draw the drapes and live in gloom.

Those who do receive it are the ones among us who remember what it means to be the helpless newborn and can give themselves over to God without condition. They do not say to themselves, "God will love me because I have made large donations to worthy causes, been a faithful spouse, and attend worship more faithfully than my neighbors." Instead, they are more likely to say, "God will love me not because of my best days but despite my worst ones." They know better than to believe they can either buy divine love or live a faithful life without it. They see the board as clear of all impediments, all defenses that otherwise might stand between themselves and God. Their creed is echoed in Scripture where Peter exhorts his followers: "Rid yourselves, therefore, of all malice, and all guile, insincerity, envy, and all slander. Like newborn infants, long for the pure, spiritual milk, so that by it you may grow into salvation—if indeed you have tasted that the Lord is good" (1 Pet. 2:1–3).

This passage paints a wonderful image in the original Greek because "spiritual milk" can also mean "sincere milk." The English word "sincere" is derived from the Italian *sine cere,* which means "without wax," and the story behind it is interesting. In ancient Rome a cup that could hold liquid without leaking was a valued commodity, and unscrupulous merchants would coat poorly crafted cups with wax to make them appear watertight. But only the pure and the unadulterated were truly *sine cere.* Peter is saying that the love we receive from God is pure, that it is a purity indicated by absence— of malice, envy, guile—and that we must be no less so. Like Holy

Communion, we come to it empty, drink from the chalice that is itself *sine cere*, and in so doing taste the kindness of the Lord.

Enduring Love

To *receive* literally means "to take back," as though we are now reclaiming a lost innocence. But even as we receive it we know that God's love does not bring with it an amnesty from pain or heartache; shadowed valleys will still be walked, we will still have enemies, and tables will still be set in their presence. Storms will still sweep to sea the shelter of the peasant while leaving intact the palace of the king. Illness will still take good people well before their time. Lonely hearts will still sit deep into the night, alone but for the ticking clock and the sleeping cat.

What is different about receiving God's love is not that it offers immunity from suffering. Instead it offers the comfort of knowing that we do not shoulder it alone. In this sense we are like that newborn baby whose primal pain can be announced only in fitful tears. He does not know its origin or meaning, but he does know that he suffers. When he is gathered up by his mother and held close, beating heart against beating heart, the soft *shhhh* of her whispered voice floating through him like a gentle breeze to cool the soul, he is comforted and quieted. Not because the one who loves him has removed that pain, but because she has shared it with him and, in gestures as wordless as his, has assured him that they will see this through together. He can only either fight her loving embrace or surrender to it. Instinctively, he surrenders, and he is becalmed.

Gratitude

It is not enough, though, just to receive this gift. We must also ask, What does this make of us? Ideally, receiving this love makes us grateful, bestows gratitude. Gratitude is the disposition we take toward the love of God and the love of others. On our part it is humbling because it implies a recognition of need—why would we be grateful to receive something of no worth to us?—and thankfulness. Just as the newborn needed to receive his mother's comfort in order to calm him, we need to receive what others have to give us and are thankful when those needs are met.

Sometimes gratitude means receiving the gift that we do not even know we need, the gift so close and commonplace that we might otherwise overlook it. We find new life growing despite the cold on a gray winter morning, and it makes *us* feel a little more alive. Young parents watch their little boy pedal his bike down the dirt road to grandmother's house for the first time without his training wheels and are grateful for his health and confidence. In both cases nature is just being nature, but when we are attentive to it, we are grateful for it and receive it accordingly. As a friend of mine once mused after an all-night study binge, as we watched dawn break over a sleepy New Haven skyline, "What do you suppose people would pay to see a sunrise if it wasn't free every single morning of our lives?"

Other times gratitude involves receiving the gifts of others, which is not always as easy as it may seem. It may be more blessed to give than to receive, but it is also easier, because giving carries its own innate gratification. It is easier to feel bigger than the person we are giving to because theirs is the need and ours is the remedy, and what this implies by extension is that those on the receiving end can feel small—so small, in fact, that we are less overwhelmed by gratitude than debt, and we are uneasy until we have paid it back.

We are invited over to a friend's house for dinner and told to bring nothing, but instead we pick up a bottle of wine or a dessert, not because we want to be generous but because it feels peculiar to us to show up empty-handed. We feel as though we must somehow pay or repay our friend's kindness rather than simply receive it.

But when we reduce giving to bartering the gesture itself becomes the first casualty, and both giver and gifted suffer. We suffer because we reinforce in ourselves the notion that we are not worthy to receive unbidden kindness, thereby demeaning ourselves, and we forget that we are beloved creatures of God. The other person suffers because we deny them the generosity of their gesture by redefining it as an obligation. Only when we feel unencumbered, empty-handed appreciation can we receive in a manner that God intends. This attitude does not ask, "How can I ever repay you?" but instead declares, "Thanks, and more thanks, and even more thanks." Like a chessboard minus its pieces, it is at one and the same moment the clearest of concepts and the most difficult to actualize.

Gratitude can also entail paradox because the humility we feel when we allow ourselves to receive, empty-handed, is a worthy feeling to hold on to when we are the ones doing the giving.

Some years ago I noticed a man begging in a New York City subway station. He had his requisite paper cup and cardboard sign that told his story of a life of hard-luck happenstances, and from time to time people would pop a few coins or a folded buck into the cup and hurry by. Those who did this did not seem to pay the man much regard, did not seem to think of him so much as a person like themselves but as a casualty of circumstances that would never befall them. He was an alien, whom they were willing to help out but whose story was likely lost on them.

After a few minutes another man came along, stopped, took some money out of his billfold, put it in the cup, and extended his hand to the beggar. They shook on the deal as if they were consummating a business transaction, the donor saying, "And have a good day, sir," smiling, and then moving on. I suppose there are any number of ways to interpret this little vignette, but I chose to see it as one man seeing in the other not his inferior but his equal.

In granting dignity to this man, this angel was as much as saying, "Neither one of us is more or less human than the other. We are both born of the same stuff and both destined for the same end. My station in life may be a result of circumstances I could control and circumstances I couldn't, and the same may be said of you. In the end, my friend, we are all alive only by the grace of God, and neither one of us can do anything but receive that grace with gratitude. It is not because I am more fortunate than you that I give you this money, nor am I in any way superior to you. Rather it is because the common bond of our emptiness does more to unite us as brothers than any definition of class or status can do to separate us as citizens."

Now, what I chose to see in this man—his manner of giving—I saw, perhaps, because it was what I needed to see. I had dropped a coin in the beggar's cup and scurried away without so much as look-ing into his eyes with either compassion or recognition.

So let yourself feel satisfaction when you do a good deed for some-one else. But remind yourself that we are no less hungry for love than those to whom we extend it. When our generosity is born of our poverty rather than our wealth—our need rather than our means—we are bound more closely to one another and more closely approach God's intention that, be we man or woman, slave or free, Jew or Gen-tile, beggar or king, we can only be grateful that God gives us life and with it the ability to affect the lives of one another.

In gratefully receiving God's grace I am one with that newborn baby who is kept alive and becalmed by the unnamed angels to whom she can only surrender. I am alive to receive the wonders of the world that are no less wondrous simply by virtue of their being common-place. I openly and freely receive the love of others and allow that love to affirm my dependency, my poverty, my emptiness, my inabil-ity to pay for that which is given to me and which sustains my life. In giving to others I am carrying that affirmation one step further by acknowledging the emptiness of *all* persons and the spiritual poverty that binds us to one another. When we do share with one another out of this common experience, the gesture becomes holy. We are doing as God would have us do. As God did, as he "emptied himself, tak-ing the form of a slave, being born in human likeness. And being found in human form, he humbled himself" (Phil. 2:7–8). So in being as God would have us be we are emptying ourselves—of ego, of pride, of desire, of expectation—so as to be in a state of utter libera-tion with one another, where giving and receiving are done freely. The board is cleared of the tools of attack and defense, the things that define our competition with one another. It is in that clarity that we have our "Aha!" moment.

Questions for Discussion

What does it mean to be spiritually poor? What is the connection between our sense of poverty and our ability to receive God's love?

How can God's love be of comfort when we are suffering? How can we embody God's love to others who are suffering?

Why is it more difficult to receive than to give?

How can receiving inform our giving?

Chapter 11

Retreat

The world is too much with us.

—Wordsworth

It Can Happen to the Best of Them

In a lecture I attended some years ago at the University of Michigan, the Buddhist writer and lecturer Ram Dass once told the story of a day-long meditation exercise his guru, Sri Neem Karoli, instructed him to participate in.

"Silence and calm for twelve consecutive hours, that was his prescription for me," he told his audience. "Apparently he felt I had been flitting around to too many places giving too many lectures on the holiness of being still. A delightful irony, all in all."

The guru had Ram sit, lotus-style, on his yoga mat and, to induce a meditative state, instructed him to begin counting to one hundred to himself.

"I'd start out slowly, really paying attention," Ram said, "but I ran into a little problem. One . . . two . . . three . . . I would count, and then, *did I remember to shut off the water in the kitchen? . . .* four . . . five *. . . maybe I should've gone to the bathroom before we started . . .* six *. . .* seven . . . eight *. . . I need to pick up a quart of milk on my way home tonight. . . .* What I call 'thought mosquitoes' buzzing around my consciousness. Suffice it to say it didn't take long for it to dawn on me that Guru Neem was onto something."

Even those who devote their lives to preaching serenity need to reclaim it for themselves from time to time. "Be still, and know that I am God," the psalmist wrote (46:10), by which he means that given all the swirls and storms and wonders and banalities and hassles and curiosities that are part of everyday living, stillness is a necessity that we treat as a luxury at our own peril. We cannot stay in the swirl forever. We need to step back. We need to retreat.

Beware That First Step

There is activity in the swirl but perspective in the retreat, and without perspective we become intent on our efforts while losing sight of our aims. I remember the story of a man who lived his whole life in a village on a mountaintop, never venturing off, and who was always stupefied when people would come from distant lands and tell him what a beautiful mountain it was. To him it was just home. Then one day, late in life, the man took ill. He was told that his only hope for survival meant leaving the village, traveling a good distance, and staying in a city hospital far away from home. He reluctantly agreed.

The man's neighbor hitched up a wagon and volunteered to transport him out of the village and on to the city, and about a half an hour after they had left the mountain's base the old man looked back with eyes as wide as saucers. "My God, what a beautiful sight," he told his neighbor. "What is it?"

"That?" the neighbor replied. "That is your mountain. That is your home."

Proximity often breeds myopia, just as, conversely, distance can provide focus. We serve a God who is at work in the world, but we know God in the stillness of our heart. Just as it is our obligation to God to be a voice in the wilderness—to do the things that make possible the coming of a just world—it is our obligation to ourselves to be silent within the wilderness of our souls, to retreat from those things outside ourselves so that our lives might be brought into focus.

The Breath of Life

While the word *retreat* may conjure up images of a distant place where people gather to think deep thoughts far away from the impingements of everyday life, a warm and welcoming place of over-grown fireplaces, old hymnals, and memorable people if forgettable food, it is also quite within our reach to, as Dag Hammarskjöld once put it, "without leaving the world, plunge into God." We can be still, and still be in the world.

I once had a patient named Margaret, a youthful, brilliant, and driven scientist whose life was long on activity but short on stillness. Margaret used her talent and determination to rise high in the ranks of what she called a "sclerotically male-dominated field of professional endeavor." I do not know if she "had it all," but she had a lot. She was in a wonderful marriage to a very caring, very successful guy with whom she had two children who they both adored in word and deed. She was a Sunday school teacher. *He* was a Sunday school teacher. They had an upscale address in the priciest neighborhood of a glamorous city, and she was genuinely, deeply appreciative of her good fortunes. She was also, by her own account, a wreck. I asked her to define "wreck."

"Do you know anything about centrifugal force?" she asked, as only she might. I explained to her that if my knowledge of physics could be converted to dynamite it would not light a match.

"Okay, a little primer. Imagine a string, say a foot long," she began. "Now imagine tying a rock to one end of the string, holding the other end between your thumb and forefinger, and spinning it, as you might a slingshot, around and around." David's slingshot came to mind.

"The rock feels as though it's pulling away from you, and that's centrifugal force, and that's what I feel like. I feel like my life is spinning and spinning, and pulling away from my core. And if I let go it'll just fly off into space."

It was a perfect image, I thought. Not emblematic of chaos or loss of control, not overwhelming or despair-inducing, but relentlessly pulling away from the core. "Centrifugal" is from the Latin *centrum fugere*, "to flee the center." Margaret's life had her unwittingly on the run, fleeing the center. I asked her if she would try a small exercise with me, and she agreed.

"Close your eyes and notice your breathing," I told her. "Notice *how* you're breathing right now, and how you've been breathing since you've been in my office. It's probably how you've been breathing since you got up this morning." She noticed. Her breaths were shallow, jagged, staccato.

"Now I want you to breathe, well, like your life depended on it," I instructed her. "Deep, rich, slow, circular breaths. Gentle arcs. Your inhale will gradually feather off and become your exhale, which will slowly taper down until you inhale again. Let's just do this for a few moments." So we did. Needless to say, Margaret found it particularly calming. The rock spun slower; the string slackened.

We spoke some about the importance of breathing as what the venerable Vietnamese monk Thich Nhat Hanh calls "the link between our body and our mind." When she opened her eyes again, we returned to the topic of how complicated her life was, how "not her own" it felt.

At session's end she thanked me, in particular for how calming she found the breathing exercise. So it came as some surprise to her when I told her I had not introduced her to the exercise to calm her down, but to make a point, and it was a point that I had not yet made.

"We did that breathing about ten minutes ago," I told her. "Just ten minutes. And now, if you notice, you've returned to your old habits. Deep gulps have become shallow gasps. I didn't show you how to breathe because I wanted to relax you as much as I wanted you to see how, once you *are* relaxed, you revert almost reflexively back to familiar patterns."

For Margaret, as for most of us, it is not about breathing, per se, it is about *consciousness*, about her being conscious of her breathing, for that is what opened her up, just as her letting it slip from her consciousness tightened and constricted her, and closed her back down again. When we devote ourselves to that which we are conscious of, everything else is secondary. As a friend of mine—a professional clown—once told me, "I may be juggling any number of objects, but at any given moment I'm only touching one of them."

Thus when a young child has fallen and scraped her knee, her father pays singular attention to her pain. In that moment while he may be juggling many things, it is the only thing he is touching. He picks her up, leads her to the bathroom, sets her down, tenderly cleans and dresses her wounds, and wipes her tears from her face. He then holds her and calms her, and makes sure she is mended and steady on her feet before he releases her back into her world. Once assured, he makes a little joke to redirect her emotional radar, she sniffles and cracks a faint smile, and off she goes. It is not surgery he has performed, but for those few moments his world is no larger than that small room, populated by only two people with one mission and no distractions.

Our days are filled with scraped knees and soccer practices, grocery lists and board meetings, schoolwork that needs to be done, dinners that need to be cooked, and shrubs that need to be pruned. They are also filled with quiet times, but that is a relative term, because even then we are usually occupied with some activity, if only the activity of relaxation. We are not a people for whom stillness comes easy.

But its very foreignness is what makes it so important, because it is in stillness that we can retreat from the day, clear the clutter from our minds, be calm, breathe deep, perhaps meditate on a small scrap of Scripture or a line from a prayer, all for the purpose of knowing that God is God. As Paul Beattie once wrote, "When my mind is still and alone with the beating of my heart, I know how much life has given me." We can pick up and go if we must, travel outward, far from home, to a remote place of retreat wherein we derive the benefits that come from new scenery. But we do well to remember that we can also travel inward, journey no farther than our breaths will take us, being perfectly still, and perfectly aware of their great circular, prayer-wheel motions that gently, soothingly, tenderly tilt us Godward.

Nor is it only in physical stillness that we can experience this petit retreat from the thrum and clutter of daily life. Sam, a photographer I know, spent several years working as a deckhand on a New York City–based tugboat. A very contemplative guy who really loved his solitude, Sam welcomed the challenge to that solitude posed by living among thirteen other crew members in spartan quarters with no privacy on a small boat that remained at sea for up to three weeks at a time and carried with it, as Sam put it, "the accumulated pungency of a large crew in a small space."

"It was very difficult to have any privacy on board, let alone find the time and place to meditate," he told me. "So I had to find other ways to clear my head and find my peace.

"Whenever I awoke—depending upon my shift it was anywhere from six in the morning to six at night—I would, with great care, tend to the tiny corner of the ship that was mine. I called it my 'monk's cell.' It had my few clothes, my fewer books, my camera equipment, and a small number of other little talismans. One by one I would pick up each item, think for just a moment about why it was important to me, and then put it neatly in its place. Because I had such a small number of things, each had a role in my life on the boat; each was in its own way important. And because I had so little privacy, what space I had took on a sacred quality. I deeply appreciated it, and everything in it.

"When I finished organizing my things I would lie on my cot and think about this enforced simplicity. Then I would give thanks, and then I would begin my work."

Thinking about Sam carving out his holy cell on the deep blue sea reminds me of a small Hasidic community not far from my home, where once a week the folks there do something similar: the way Sam set aside space, they set aside time, and make it holy. It is their Sabbath, and, like a rowboat in a regatta, the Hasids in their material simplicity provide a welcome counterpoint to a city driven by glitz, glitter, grandeur, and the relentless pursuit of commerce.

Enter their neighborhood on a sunny Saturday afternoon and you hear no horns or music, see no automobile traffic, no shops open for business, no restaurants offering two-for-one mimosa-laced brunch specials. Instead you see people by the hundreds, clusters of family and friends, all modestly dressed in colorless clothes meant to conceal rather than reveal, all walking with absolutely no air of urgency about them to some nearby destination that, whatever else transpires, will be a place of reflection and rest. There is a pervasive calm in the air as the community gathers to honor the fourth commandment. On this day they rest, as God rested, and by doing as God did they keep it holy.

A wise rabbi once described it for me: "Over the years, with all that we have endured, more than the Jews have kept the Sabbath, the Sabbath has kept the Jews." In weekly retreat from the world as they daily know it, they are kept whole. Like Margaret with her breathing or Sam carving out his little corner of solid ground on the high seas, it is not just the act of rest they are engaged in but the awareness, the consciousness, they bring to it. Cleared of any distractions, they are attentive to the day, feeling the friendship around them, experiencing their rest as a mirror to the heavens, where God himself is also at rest. "Be still, and know that I am God." So they are, and thusly they know.

Retreat as Prologue

To paraphrase the great scholar Martin Buber, we cannot exist our whole lives in retreat, but without it we can *only* exist. Without the recuperative powers of attentive quietude our days become defined by activities that, however worthy, are insufficient to a spiritual life. We must also be fed. Nevertheless, it was only one day that God rested, not seven. We retreat not solely to remove ourselves *from* the world but also to better prepare ourselves for what it means to live *in* it.

A forester friend once asked me if I understood why leaves shrivel on trees when they do not receive sufficient water. Given that I am no more conversant at botany that I am at physics, I confessed that while it just looked to me as though the leaves are dying, I could not begin to explain the dynamics of botanical death.

"Actually," she said, "it's subtler than that. It's not so much dying as it is trying very hard to live. The leaf 'understands' that the sun is the culprit here, so, like a child hiding from the bogeyman, it purposely makes itself as small as it can. It knows that the more of its surface area it exposes to the sun, the quicker it will dry out, so it gives the sun as small a target as possible. It retreats, if you will, until it can get the sustenance it needs, after which it opens itself again, and goes about doing its job of being a leaf."

I may not know science, but I know a good metaphor when I hear one. The living waters we receive in the stillness of retreat are the sustenance we need for our return to the world. The place that God spent the first six days creating, the place we call the earth and the fullness thereof, is in constant need of our love, and, like the nourished leaf, we return to her larger and stronger, to the end that we may go about doing our job as people of faith.

This is what Margaret wanted to get to when she opened her eyes again. When we do go back to the world at hand we want to see that it can look different, if but a little bit. Quiet can be heard just as stillness can be felt. The lilies of the field can be considered, the lion can be seen lying down with the lamb, and those who mourn can be blessed and comforted. Beauty is beheld in an ordinary houseplant, and wisdom is found hidden in the rambling observations made by a young child in his fourth-grade book report. Like God himself we survey the wonders of creation and declare them to be good.

They are good because when we open our eyes again we are better. If someone is hurtful to us—be it someone we like, dislike, or do not even know—we know that the hurt is better met with compassion than resentment. Perhaps it is not a good day for them, we think. Perhaps they have just received some bad news. Or perhaps it is nothing of the sort and there is no good excuse for their behavior. But we remember that they are still God's creatures, that we are as capable of the same small-mindedness that must be met with large-heartedness, and that we gain nothing by bringing pain to pain.

When we think of the things that make for a better creation, a more just society, or even simply a home in which peace prevails over conflict, we feel newly inspired to make whatever contributions we can to turn the possibility into certainty. We harbor no illusion that our world is suddenly purged of deep, disturbing problems, that in many instances the depth of those problems is attributable to the shallowness of human imagination, and that we will not solve them without sacrifice and sweat. But we are also hopeful, as the disciples were on that first Christian Sabbath when, in the face of an empty tomb, they knew the enormous impediments that lay before them but knew too that this tomb spoke of nothing if it did not first speak of hope. If that one stone could be moved, others could as well.

So, with eyes open, in the words of the old hymn, "awake to love and work," we do both. We love and we work. We bring to both tasks the patience of the ages, the centeredness of the mystics, and the persistence of the saints. We care for those who either cannot or will not care for themselves. We right wrongs, however slight, that we may have had a hand in, however small. We practice better stewardship both of the world and of our own lives, offer unbidden apologies, and forgive those who do not even ask for it. For we are feeling generous, and, to paraphrase Edmund Wilson, generosity only grows when we give it away.

We do all this knowing that time and circumstance are arrayed against us, that angers lie hiding in the weeds eager to stay us from our course, and that at some point a predictable accumulation of disappointments and sadnesses will, like running water on a resting stone, slowly erode our resolve. We know this because the world is not perfect and neither are we. Our deep breaths will grow fitful again, the centrifugal force of our collective obligations will pull our center askew. We will return a slight with a hard stare as patience cedes ground to judgment, which itself will be neither cool nor openhearted, but stingy and self-serving. That is when it is time again to retreat, time to "be still, and know that I am God," because in some small way we will have forgotten this. Retreat is not an acquaintanceship that, once made, we need not visit again. It is a core place that we return to when the circumstances of life and the busyness of living inevitably conspire—as is their wont—to distract us from that core.

On a Grander Scale

Given the personal, interior nature of retreat, it may seem odd to think about the principles of retreat being pertinent to world affairs, but I sometimes wonder if the brinksmanship that underscores so much of politics and industry might be avoided if leaders stepped back now and again, looked inside themselves, and took a breath.

When, for instance, young men and women killed in battle are referred to as "collateral damage," I am outraged, not only because the phrase has such a dehumanizing ring to it but because this is the intention behind its use. It is meant to minimize the cost of war by sanitizing its barbarity. When industry giants maximize their profits at the expense of our rivers and air, or fire thousands of workers and still take home seven-figure bonuses, or eviscerate the pension plan that was those workers' only hope for retirement, I seethe at the unmitigated, unconscionable hubris they display, their arrogance nothing less than a callous disregard for anything beyond the satisfaction of their own pleasures or the stroking of their own egos. I wish they were ignorant of the suffering they have caused rather than indifferent toward it because stupidity is more forgivable than venality.

What is it if not hubris that drives such people to remember only the privileges of power and forget its responsibilities? I believe they would do well to retreat, to step back, so that they might, like the old man on the mountain, truly see the frail beauty of the earth and all that is in it. I believe they would be humbled by it, be stilled by it, know that God is God, and, more importantly, that they are not. A little humility in the service of humanity is not a lot to ask of those to whom much has been entrusted and therefore much expected, and retreat is a good first step, because while it is a personal experience it has public consequences. We do not retreat to avoid our responsibility to creation but to better assume it.

Coming and Going

At its best retreat is not an occasion of removal so much as a habit of the heart. Just as the withered leaf needs more than a moment's replenishment or the body needs more than one deep breath, retreat is a place we return to, the way an infant returns to her mother's breast for sustenance that is both essential and provisional.

With this in mind we are wise to anticipate our needs before they are upon us, to reach for the breath before we are winded, to take our stillness before the forces of life have yanked us from our center, to know that God is God before we have forgotten that this is so. Just as the overtired child can never sleep but fitfully, we do ourselves no favor if we take our rest only after discovering that we are spiritually exhausted. The leaf can protect itself only so long.

Instead we serve ourselves—and by inference, our God—when even a little stillness becomes an everyday occurrence. The wristwatch comes off, the telephone is unplugged, the lights are dimmed, the dinner can wait. We close our eyes to the world and are alone with our thoughts. Even these we let go of, because they will be there waiting for us when we return. We are, as Beattie said it, alone with the beating of our heart, and the circles of our breaths. Inhaling and exhaling, drawing in and letting go, journey inward and journey outward. We discover that in this simple rhythm there can be found the essence of life itself: the rhythm of give and take, of receiving and relinquishing, of living and dying and living again. It is God calling us to this sacred home, this home that can be found in as unlikely a place as a tugboat's dark hold just as easily as behind the darkness of our closed eyes. It is God whispering to us, *Come to me, all you that are weary and carrying heavy burdens, and I will give you rest* (Matt. 11:28). *Peace I leave with you; my peace I give to you* (John 14:27). *Come home with me and dine* (1 Kgs. 13:7). *Be still, and know that I am God* (Ps. 46:10). It is all this, and more. And it is us, listening.

Questions for Discussion

What are some of the things you need to take retreat from? How can you be replenished? How does retreat help you to return to those things?

How can we retreat and remain in the world? What techniques are useful to us? What role does consciousness play?

What did the juggler mean when he said, "I may be juggling any number of objects, but at any given moment I'm only touching one of them"?

How can we build little "retreat moments" into our everyday lives?

Chapter 12

Revival

Not a soul takes thought how well he may live—only how long; yet a good life might be everybody's, a long one can be nobody's.

—Seneca

Friday Afternoon at the Old Bodega

It is just after four on a Friday afternoon, which explains the long line outside Angelo's Bodega on East 106th Street in New York City. It is payday at Mount Sinai Hospital, a few steps away, and for some of the workers Angelo's is their first stop. These are not the doctors, therapists, or administrators on whose shoulders the hospital's public reputation sits. No, these are the folks who work in the laundry room or the cafeteria, the custodians who mop floors and empty wastebaskets, the aides who change sheets and scrub bedpans, the secretaries and receptionists who are the first line of attack for angry patients or irate family members. They are the largely invisible employees, today very visible as they wait patiently on line, not to purchase food or beverage but to indulge their impossible dream. For it is Friday afternoon, and we are just hours away from something called the New York State Mega-Million Dollar Lottery drawing. They are buying their tickets.

Emil, a janitor, steps up to the window. Short and stocky, with smoky eyes, a tattoo of the Virgin Mary on one forearm and a stiletto on the other, and something less than his full complement of teeth, Emil flashes a smile of familiarity at the man behind the counter.

"Gimmie two Quick Picks a Take Five and a Mega Million with a bonus, Jimmie." His total is $6.00 for the day. Later, he tells me he spends about $20 to $30 a week, a little over a thousand dollars a year from a $35,000 salary on "the game," and while he has not hit the big one just yet (Emil's odds are roughly seven *billion* to one), he is still holding out hope. As with many of his colleagues on line, rumor has it that a friend of a friend's older sister's first husband's second cousin cleaned up a few years ago, so why not him?

I am not so much struck by Emil and his coworkers looking for the big score—after all, we all have a little "Rocky" in us—as I am by the deadened tone with which they stand in line and place their orders. "Three Back Deuce square seven on Lotto three power four on the High Ball . . . Six Quick Picks double four three bonus mega . . . Pick Ten Win Four two no limits a Cash 'n Flash and three—no, make it four—Juicy Loots." It is a language intelligible only to the initiated, delivered in a flat voice, keen on precision born of endless repetition and low on feeling. I would think that someone laying out their hard-earned cash on a chance to pocket the equivalent of about a thousand years' income would do so with a little more brio, but that is not the case.

If it is hope that has brought them here, it is not the kind of hope found in, say, the quavering voice of a bride-to-be or the steely-eyed stare of a baseball manager whose team is mounting a late-game comeback. Instead what comes across is more a commentary on luck and life, a weary, weekly ritual engaged in by people, many of whom are used to going up against long odds. They are here because there is something more they want out of life, yet they are lacking passion because they doubt very much that this will give it to them. They more closely resemble Dryden's observation, "When I consider life, 'tis all a cheat; yet, fool'd with hope, men favor the deceit."

When I ask Emil why he plays—why he "favors the deceit"—he just shrugs, tells me, "Same reason a lot of people without much money play. Because we're lousy at math," and flashes me a grin that resembles a picket fence with a couple of slats missing. I suspect there is more to it than this, though; perhaps it is an unconscious but unshakable desire to get something for nothing, or perhaps it is that the lure of the siren's exceptionally faint and faded *maybe* is so impenetrable by reason. After all, it is a *maybe* overheard often in their workplace, spoken by doctors or clergy talking to desperate patients and anxious families: a hope against hope, a belief that sometimes miracles do happen, because they once did, to a friend of a friend's older sister's. . . .

I am quite certain there is more to life for Emil and for the others like him on this long line of dreamers. I am sure many have families they love and children they can rightfully brag about, modest homes well kept with little gardens carefully tended. Many are proud of the work that they do—as well they should be—and the industriousness they bring to their labors. There are friendships that stretch back many years, faithful attendance at Sunday mass, and donations of time and talent to causes near to their hearts. This one ritual at Angelo's Bodega does not define them, but it does define a piece of them, and perhaps a piece of all of us.

There are times when we hope for something that we no longer believe will come our way (perhaps we never did), times when hope is hollow but we are not yet ready to admit our resignation, not yet ready to pull ourselves off the line of doubtful dreamers. We still strain to hear the faint *maybe*. It is at times like these that we are not fully alive because we are not engaged in the activity that is, at that moment and of our own volition, consuming our time. It is a pretense, a kind of going-through-the-motions ennui hovering around a behavior that might have once meant something to us but no longer does.

I watch a friendship of many years not so much break up as slowly dissipate, and not because of animosity or betrayal but because habit has so gotten the better of enthusiasm that the friends, both of whom may very much love life apart from each other, now feel emotionally suffocated in each other's presence. Or I see a person who at one time held a fervent faith gradually let go, piece by piece, of all things spiritual in her life because the effort no longer seems proportionate to the return. Suddenly one day she realizes that there is little left beyond an occasional, guilt-induced trip to worship, where her prayers are rote and her attention is divided. When during the service the congregation sings the old Henry Butler hymn, "Lift Up Your Hearts," she realizes that hers will not budge, and that her time within those hallowed halls may be limited.

The fact is, any number of things that once lifted us up can then wear us down. The friend who once made us laugh has grown tiresome, the job that promised security delivers tedium, the principles we once marched for in candlelight vigil have grown quaint as we have aged our way into prickly skepticism. We may ask ourselves what has changed, but of course it is we who have changed, have lost some of our optimism, and have contented ourselves with living partial lives.

Revive Us Again

Psalm 85 reads as an exquisitely plaintive cry over a once-favored civilization that is now lost and looking to find its way back home again. In its earliest verses we hear the sad song of a people in exile whose God was once, long ago, "favorable to [his] land," who "restored the fortunes of Jacob," who "forgave the iniquity of [his] people," and who "withdrew all [his] wrath." These reminiscences then give way to their one simple plea: "Revive us again, O God of our salvation"—*re viviere*, literally, bring us back to life—a revival in which "faithfulness will spring up from the ground, and righteousness will look down from the sky."

It is the tale of a life once lived with gratitude that gave way to expectation, a sense of appreciation for a privileged existence that yielded to a sense of entitlement that such was their birthright. This was the iniquity that the God of second chances once forgave and is being asked to forgive once more, as the psalmist entreats his God to "revive us *again*."

I do not think of the people's sins—their "iniquities"—as having necessarily been egregious transgressions against divine law. I think it is entirely possible that they simply settled into a kind of emotional torpor, a religious listlessness, a lack of passion for the gift of life. When this happens, good things do not ensue. We are afforded only one spin on the carousel, and I do not believe God wants us distracted or indifferent when we take it. Perhaps it was this indifference that exiled the people of this psalm (be it spiritually or physically) from the God who had bestowed so much on them.

Perhaps this is why their faithfulness did not now spring forth to meet God's righteousness.

That said, though, the psalm is also a people's first step toward reviving that faithfulness because in it they recognize the gifts that God has given them, imply their inattentiveness to those gifts, acknowledge that they are spiritually lifeless, and finally, in a passage of intimate beauty and aching hope, look forward again, to a day when "steadfast love and faithfulness will meet; [and] righteousness and peace will kiss each other." In an irony so emblematic of the human condition, when the land was theirs and the people were flush they grew indifferent to their riches, but only when they lived at the hand of another and deprivation was the order of the day could they again believe in a God of salvation and deliverance.

It Is Less Our Life Than How We See Our Life

The psalmist's exile is ours as well to the extent that our passion for life is compromised by our carelessness toward it. When joys become habits or impediments become blockades, our lives themselves are reduced to shadow—all motion without meaning, dark space without substance, it leaves behind no lasting impression when it has passed. Our land of milk and honey, our Canaan, that metaphorical state of grace in which we experience life like "the fortunes of Jacob," is replaced with a sense of estrangement. At our best our hands might rise pleadingly to the heavens, but at our worst our shoulders shrug, apathetic, as though waiting without expectation, like Beckett's clowns, for the Godot who will not materialize, the phantom lottery ticket that is the answer to all of our problems.

If in our estrangement we are to be brought back to life, it will be less because the circumstances of our lives change than that our perceptions of them do. I once worked with a woman named Evelyn who was deeply involved in her vocation as a social justice advocate but whose commitment was not so much an expression of passion as it was a sublimation of deep-seated, years-old pain. Her wake-up call came, of all places, at one of the endless meetings she was expected to attend as part of her contribution to an antiracism campaign.

"At one point during the meeting," she told me, "I stood up, and quietly asked the others not to mind me, I was just a little uncomfortable sitting. They pressed me on it—gently, but insistently—and I finally explained that I had a form of cancer that I was being treated for, and the chemo treatments made it difficult for me to remain seated for long stretches.

"Without saying anything at all, three of them got up out of their chairs and came over to me. One of them closed my laptop. Another gathered my papers. The third helped me on with my coat. 'You go home and rest,' they instructed me. 'Your work will get done; we'll see to that. You now have other, more important work to tend to.'

"And so I did, and from that point on I came to look at work differently, and, when I recovered, I looked at life differently, more gratefully. Work no longer defines me, and small gestures like my 'enforced convalescence' have come to mean the world to me. I now refer to those folks as my three wise men, my magi. They came to me unexpectedly, bearing gifts of unimaginable worth, and asking nothing in return. I am so thankful for them."

Evelyn's was a life in limbo despite outward appearances of fullness and comfort, but just as it was her pain that opened the gateway to her revival, it is for many others the inconsolable, indescribable, unremitting pain of life that is their greatest obstacle. JoAnn Anderson is one of the legion of lifelong, blue-collar New Orleanians who, when Hurricane Katrina came and took away her city, lost her home, her belongings, her hopes, and her job as well. In her mid-fifties, with twenty-two years of hotel housekeeping under her belt, she is now considered too old to employ and cannot find work in the neighborhood of Memphis where she and her longtime companion were relocated after the storm. But she is also too young to collect a pension or social security, so she stands in a kind of hinterland where she cannot stand forever.

"I was born poor; I'm probably going to die poor," she told a reporter. Where once she had an affordable apartment with a touch of character in an uptown New Orleans neighborhood that was accessible to her job at a Garden District hotel, she now lives among strangers in a monochromatic, FEMA-subsidized apartment complex with an empty swimming pool and frayed ropes that dangle where children's swings once stood. She has no car and so must walk a long distance to the economy grocery store, where, for the first time in her life, she purchases her groceries with food stamps.

"I want to work," she said to the reporter. "I don't want to just sit around getting my bones all old and everything." But what she wants out of life and what life will give her may be two different things, so for people like JoAnn, people for whom calamity has made life a series of crises to endure and indignities to overcome, a broader, loving community must step to the fore. For hers is the story that reminds us that we are all dependent upon one another, that one person's misery is every person's burden, and that the physical declination of one human being's life signals the moral diminution of all our lives. The psalmist did not pray, "revive *me* again," but "revive *us* again."

JoAnn's story and the countless others like hers is the reminder (Why must we always be reminded?) that vitality suffuses a community only if it looks after the least within its ranks. We are the ones who can offer the second chance, the job, the daycare, the education, the extra groceries, the lenient loan, the passageway to dignity, and then watch the loaves and fishes miracle by which the physical ascent of one human being's life signals the moral expansion of all our lives. It is not only sinful to see one of our own be forced to sit around getting her bones all old, it is unnecessary.

Of Slings and Scars

They are legion and sometimes cunning, these saboteurs that bend us toward lives, as Eliot's Prufrock's, "measured out like coffee spoons." They afflict people of wealth or want, people social or solitary, people prone to ponder deep things and others who simply make it up as they go along. One person might have become jaded early in her days by violated confidences or misplaced trusts and, over years, come to view so many people with suspicion that now she cannot fully love life for fear that it will mean collapsing the walls that have separated her from human contact but also shielded her from further hurt. Another may have realized his long-held dream to accumulate jazzier, flashier, and costlier toys than anyone else on the block, only to discover that playing with them brings only diminishing returns, and that for some strange reason the real thrill was in the hunt, not the conquest.

For another the wound is deeper, when a life well lived to the glory of God and in obedience to God's will is rewarded by a debilitating accident, a crippling illness, or the premature death of a loved one. It is so very difficult for her to turn again to this God for revival, this God whom she long worshiped as her rock and her salvation but whom she now cannot help but see, as Job did, as the heartless perpetrator of a cruel joke.

None of us goes through life unscathed. Over the years chips and chunks are taken out of us. We become accustomed to things that used to enchant us, inured to things that used to inflame us, or skeptical about things that used to inspire us. Revival is hard work, which is why the psalmist spoke for an entire people when he beseeched God's help to renew the weary bodies and refresh the parched souls of a people whose lives were now half lived. It is not something we do easily alone.

But surrender is not something that we need to succumb to. Imagination bolstered by faith (and perhaps seasoned with a little risk) can be brought to bear on a lifeless life such that, with the sublime guidance of a God whose very name means "Being," we can throw off the old warning that the only difference between a rut and a grave is depth, and we can be revived. The man who has lived for himself his whole life can pick up a hammer and build a house for JoAnn Anderson, just as JoAnn can give herself the gift of allowing the community to support her in her need. The woman for whom church no longer seems to be filling the bill can remind herself that there is a difference between religion and faith, that there are times when the former stultifies rather than invigorates the latter, and that she can commune with God on her own terms. The workaholic can show the courage needed to look into his own heart and face up to the demons that drive his overwhelming need for works righteousness. Those who have suffered great tragedy can give themselves wide latitude to be angry—a pulse quickener if ever there was one—with circumstances that have worked against them, or friends who have disappointed them, or a God who has seemed silent to them. For it is only in latching on to that anger that they will eventually be able to transform it into something life affirming.

In this last regard I think of an extraordinarily strong woman by the name of Lisa Ramaci, an art critic and the widow of freelance journalist Steven Vincent, who with his Iraqi translator, Nour al-Khal, was kidnapped, shot, and given up for dead in Basra in August of 2005. Al-Khal survived, but because of her association with Vincent her life was in grave and constant danger. Ramaci took up her cause, and after eighteen months of writing, calling, and cajoling government officials, she somehow managed to win asylum for al-Khal. Not only that, but the bond of sadness and the cause of justice is so great between them that they now live together in Ramaci's small Greenwich Village apartment. Now, the American art critic and the Iraqi translator devote themselves to advocacy work on behalf of Iraqi refugees and the families of Iraqis killed while working with American journalists.

Lisa Ramaci surely lost a piece of her own life when her husband died, and I have no doubt that the months following were peppered with every imaginable emotion from white rage to lightless grief. I also have no doubt that together with Nour al-Khal, she is revived, alive again, perhaps like never before.

Most of us will be spared the unimaginable suffering that is the legacy of war, but the kind of reawakening that makes life fresh and calls our attention to little gifts long overlooked can come to us in ways that, while short on drama, can nonetheless be long on wisdom. Many years ago, when I was serving as a minister to a university community, a small group of students came to me to register a gripe and solicit my help. Each of these students, in his or her own way, lived with some form of physical handicap, and their patience was wearing thin with the cheap snickers and bad jokes they endured at the hands of some of their physically whole if emotionally stunted classmates.

One of the responses we fashioned to their dilemma was to get each of the members of the school's student senate to agree to spend one entire day in a wheelchair, surrender all use of their legs for twenty-four hours, and then be willing to talk to a broader audience of their experience. As we expected, when they first took possession of their chairs there was a lot of drag racing, wheel popping, and lame, late-adolescent humor. But it did not take long for them to notice the building that was not handicap accessible, the lunch line that they could not manage with both their chair and their food tray, the bathroom that took feats of contortionism to utilize, the classroom whose floor was sloped, the window that was too high for them to look out of, the stares of the able-bodied, even, as one of them told me, the shoes that would be worn lifelong without so much as a good scuff.

The next day, when they were ready to get back on their feet, one of them, a young man named Zach, asked first that his picture be taken in the chair. He said he wanted a constant reminder of the things he takes for granted, and without the photograph he feared he would soon store this experience in the recesses of his mind, thinking little of it, if at all, in years to come. We obliged him. When he then stood up and took his first step his vision was ever so slightly blurred by the tiniest hint of a tear in his eye. He said he planned to spend a good bit of the day on his feet.

More than twenty years later, Zach is fully grown to adulthood. I hope he still has the photograph and that he still allows himself to be reminded. Perhaps, I think, he is somewhere on a line, on his feet, well-scuffed shoes, like the folks at Angelo's, waiting for something miraculous to happen. If so, I hope it dawns on him that it has already happened. He has won the prize. He is alive, his faithfulness caressed by God's righteousness, revived again, by this God of second chances, this God who is there, standing with him, and was so the whole time.

Questions for Discussion

What do we need revival from? What are the things in life that deaden us?

Is it possible to revive old relationships that have gone stale? Is it sometimes better to let them die a good death?

How can dramatic, even life-threatening, situations revive us?

How can members of a faith community provide revival for one another?

A Brief Concluding Musing

Everything that grows holds in perfection but a little moment.
—Shakespeare

Good people are good because they've come to wisdom through failure. We get very little wisdom from success, you know.
—William Saroyan

For what it is worth, bumper stickers are not everybody's choice as the most expressive method at our disposal for exercising our First Amendment rights. Beyond the few that are poignant, thoughtful, or downright hilarious, many of us just are not interested in asking anyone about their grandchildren, do not need to know that someone ❤s their Lhasa Apso, and really do not care that their other car is a Rolls Royce. In the eyes of some this form of announcing ourselves has a shameless self-promotional quality to it, one that seems to insist on foisting on one person's sensibilities another's doctrine on anything from politics to Pampers to personal piety.

Piety. A particularly tough bumper crop, in part because humility is its cornerstone, and humility, by its very nature, is not something we do well to advertise. That said, there is one bumper sticker that, despite its somewhat treacly quality and air of smugness, is worthy of some attention. *"Christians Aren't Perfect, Just Forgiven!"* it reads, although Christians—or any other religious communion, for that matter—have no more cornered the market on forgiveness than

Republicans have on family values. Still, there is a subtle wisdom to this sentiment that may even be lost on its author.

Religiously speaking, perfection is something we aspire to but never attain, and forgiveness is something we attain even if we don't aspire to it. No feeling person can ponder even for a moment this glorious place we call Mother Earth without being left breathless by the grandeur of a great mountain range or the beauty of a fragile daylily that grows along its steep sides, the vastness of an ocean or the flawless synchronicity made evident in the setting of the sun, the changing of the seasons, or the hatching of a wren's egg. If nature does not inspire a sense of perfection, then nothing does, but even nature in all of its fecund majesty is hardly a place we humans would deem flawless.

As Annie Dillard points out, why, for instance, must the lowly puffball go through the trouble of manufacturing and dispensing tens of thousands of tiny spores just so that a few dozen might take root, and of those few dozen only a handful will themselves grow enough to reproduce? Why is the balance in nature so precarious that a tiger with six teats and seven cubs will abandon the weakest to die a slow and painful death? What purposes do aphids serve, and why can't those purposes be served by something that does not destroy vegetables, fruits, and the plants that bear them? Does a housefly suffer when it is snared in the death grip of the spider's web, or a wildebeest in the jaws of a lion? How is any of this an intimation of perfection?

Even though it can be a rough place redolent with arbitrary pain, wanton waste, and recurring mistakes, when we look at nature as God's work we still think Edenic thoughts. But if Eden is our ideal, perhaps we do well to remember that even it came with a caveat. "It's all yours, and it's all good," God as much as told its first and last tenants, "except. . . ." For there amid beauty and bounty and "every tree that is pleasant to the sight and good for food" (Gen. 2:9), right in the middle of the garden, was the single tree that was at one and the same time the most tempting and the most deadly. This is perfection?

If in only some vaguely platonic way we can conceive of perfection (the garden without the lethal tree), we are afforded something on which to affix our sites without ever expecting to actually capture it. "Be perfect, therefore, as your heavenly Father is perfect" (Matt. 5:48), Jesus instructs us, knowing full well that he was sent to earth precisely because we are inveterate imperfectionists and always will be. As Samuel Johnson put it, "It is reasonable to have perfection in our eye, that we may always advance towards it, though we know it can never be reached." There is nobility in the quest, if futility in the outcome, and we do well to remember that it is to noble things and good causes that we are called.

What does it mean to seek the perfect as imperfect beings? It is to work for peace all the while knowing that however often we beat our swords into plowshares they will in time be beaten back into swords again, and it is loving your enemies even though you will never make them your friends. To be imperfect and seek the perfect is to live a life of material generosity in which we give of ourselves enough to feel the pain of deprivation but probably not so much that we will allow ourselves to be as threadbare, hungry, and shoeless as those who are the beneficiaries of that generosity. It is also the struggle to give up that nagging need we have to be told how generous we are. In seeking the perfect we love our child no less for striking out with the bases loaded but gird ourselves for the fact that he will not be quite so merciful with himself, and his derogation is more representative of how our culture treats success and failure than is our compassion. The pursuit of perfection is the swim against an eternal tide that is always stronger than our strength but is worth taking on because to do so promises us some headway, and not to do so promises only to send us eddying back in the wrong direction.

We live in a world where life teems but spores and tiger cubs and soldiers and innocent bystanders die unnecessarily, a place abundant enough to feed twice its current population but morally incapable of keeping a third of its citizens from going to bed hungry every night. It is a bedazzling, bedeviling place that, for better or for worse, we humans have been given dominion over. Knowing that it is as imperfect as we are, we are wise to approach that dominion with a sense of mission and a measure of humility.

Forgiveness Has a Human Face

I once had a patient named Sammy who was a real perfectionist. Sammy was a carpenter, a member of the Teamsters. He had the soul of a poet and the body of a linebacker, and, fearful of ever making a mistake, *any* mistake, he agonized over even the smallest decisions in his life. One night in my office I used his profession to try and make a point.

"Sammy," I asked him, "what do you call that woodwork at the base of my office walls, where the wall meets the floor?"

Meeting stupidity with politeness, he patiently explained, "That's your molding. It's decorative."

"But why is it there?" I asked.

"It's there essentially to cover up the gap between where the wall and the floor meet. There's always a little gap, and it doesn't look so hot, so we use molding."

"Ah, I see," I said. "In other words, in carpentry, when you can't make a perfect fit, you make accommodations. The molding is a kind of accommodation for the fact that you can't make the perfect fit between the wall and the floor. Am I getting it right?"

"Exactly."

We then paused for a moment. The room was silent. Then Sammy, breaking out into a kind of slow-motion, Cheshire-cat grin, looked at me, chuckled, and said, "Okay, no need to hit me over the head with a two-by-four. I get it."

We need not be perfect, not when we can be forgiven, or accommodated, or compromised with, or otherwise provided a second chance to right a wrong. But nor do we serve ourselves or others if we willfully mistake forgiveness for dismissiveness, as if voluntary moral diligence is a byproduct of profound neurotic guilt. A life of faith is not a life exemplary of ideals but it is a life committed to those ideals. They are our grail, our moral compass, the direction toward which we, in some erratic and serpentine manner, slowly march. Along the way, we get lost, but are given direction. We tire, but are given sustenance. We doubt, but are given fortitude. We are distracted by something more appealing or less arduous, but are given wisdom and discipline. We persevere and are given encouragement. We fall short, and are afforded the second chance. All along the way we notice that others around us have fallen short as well, struggling to bear up and carry on. There is comfort in this, because it reminds us that falling short is a common condition rather than a singular disorder, indicative not of discrete pathology but of universal humanity.

In a moment of crystal clarity we realize that it is God's justice that summons us to those ideals, just as it is God's mercy that supports us in the times when, to paraphrase Marian Wright Edelman, the waters are wide, our boat is small, our resources scarce, our will depleted. It is not mercy that we need to seek, because mercy is divinely bestowed. Like the air that we breathe, mercy is there because we need it, because we need to draw it into ourselves. It is life-giving, sustaining; it resists our resistance.

"Be perfect, therefore. . . ." We see God's will if only through a glass darkly, but even that darkened image is clear enough to guide our eyes and steer our hearts toward the ideal. For ultimately it is we who must live the lives of justice and mercy. We are the ones who must point ourselves toward perfection, acknowledge when we have wandered far afield of it, as inevitably we will, again, and again, and again, and then accept the equally persistent invitation to return and carry on.

When we have forgotten that "a wandering Aramean was my ancestor" (Deut. 26:5), we can be made to remember because Deuteronomy will remind us of our roots as a rootless people to the end that we show greater compassion to those among us who have no home. When demonic forces conspire to thwart our hopes or dash our dreams, we will remember Job; and like him, good friends will gather around us to commiserate. And hopefully, unlike him, they will offer comfort without judgment. In the warmth of their love we will be restored. The petty pressures of the day-to-day may leave us spiritually parched, but in due course the Sabbath will come, as God commanded we will treat it as holy, will use it to retreat from the pedantries of life, will slake our thirst for things righteous, and will again be mindful of the difference between being in the world and being of it. In ways too numerous to mention, whether mediated by a mighty clap of thunder or the whispered secret of a little child, God confirms Kierkegaard's assertion that we need never be without hope, that the only real sin is despair. The second chance is always within reach, ours for the taking.

But it is ours for the giving as well, for our faith is made manifest in receiving God's grace but made stronger in reflecting it. It is within our power to forgive old slights and new hurts, to lift the flagging spirits of a person we care about or extend a loving gesture to the person no one cares about. We can use our money and our muscle to help in the resurrection of a blighted neighborhood, or volunteer our efforts to revive a failing school, or spend time showing a jaded teenager that even in the torrent and turbulence that is adolescence, life can still present its enchantments. We too can be the givers of second chances, the instruments of infinite possibility.

In the end it may all be about possibility. On any given day, in any given endeavor, we may get it right, may think and feel and live in accordance with God, may have our will align with the will of the Divine. It is always possible, and it is always up to us. There is strength in knowing that we are capable of doing such a thing and comfort in knowing that when we fail we will be righted and asked to try again by a God who never stops believing in us. We are not perfect. But we are forgiven.